Retail A~~~~

Management

Retail Area
Management

STRATEGIC AND LOCAL MODELS
FOR DRIVING GROWTH

CHRIS EDGER

LIBRI
PUBLISHING

First published in 2016 by Libri Publishing

Copyright © Chris Edger

ISBN 978 1 909818 88 0

A CIP catalogue record for this book is available from The British Library

Cover design by Helen Taylor

Design by Helen Taylor

Printed in the UK by Henry Ling Limited

Libri Publishing
Brunel House
Volunteer Way
Faringdon
Oxfordshire
SN7 7YR

Tel: +44 (0)845 873 3837

www.libripublishing.co.uk

ABOUT THE AUTHOR

Dr Chris Edger is the author of *Effective Multi-Unit Leadership – Local Leadership in Multi-Site Situations* (described by the *Leadership and Organisation Development Journal* as 'one of the key books of its kind for this decade'), *International Multi-Unit Leadership – Developing Local Leaders in International Multi-Site Operations*, *Professional Area Management – Leading at a Distance in Multi-Unit Enterprises* (1st and 2nd editions), *Franchising – How Both Sides Can Win* (shortlisted for the 2016 CMI Management Book of the Year Award) and *Effective Brand Leadership – Be Different. Stay Different. Or Perish!* Since 2010 Chris has been Professor of Multi-Unit Leadership at Birmingham City Business School (BCBS). He has also taught at the University of Birmingham and the Warwick Business School, where he is the winner of several teaching excellence awards on the Warwick MBA Programme.

Chris has over 20 years of senior leisure and retail multi-unit operations, sales and support expertise working for domestic and internationally owned multi-site service companies. During his career he has held area management and regional operations director (400+ units) positions. In addition he has held executive board positions as Group HRD, Commercial Director and Sales Managing Director in organisations with multi-site interests in China, Eastern Europe and Germany. He has been a member of an executive management team that transacted two major cross-border M&A deals that totalled £2.3 billion and $1.7 billion, respectively.

His specialist teaching areas on the MSc in Multi-Unit Leadership and Strategy at BCBS are Service Leadership and Operational Improvement within retail, hospitality and leisure multi-unit contexts. Described by some commentators as the UK's leading expert on 'multi-site retail management', Chris frequently features in the media having appeared on and/or written for outlets such as Channel 4 News, ITV, BBC News Online, City A.M., Propelinfo, The Retail Gazette, *Daily Mail, Guardian, Telegraph, Retail Week, Drapers* etc. Chris holds a PhD (ESRC Award) from Warwick Business School, an MSc (econ) with distinction from the London School of Economics, an MBA from NBS and a Level 7 Advanced Coaching and Mentoring Award from the CIPD.

CONTENTS

Section 3 – EXECUTE Blueprint and Plan   81

Section 4 – EVOLVE Operations and Offer   121

Section 5 – AM Personal Characteristics   151

THIS BOOK IS DEDICATED TO THE HUNDREDS OF GENERAL MANAGERS, AREA MANAGERS, OPERATIONS DIRECTORS AND SENIOR SUPPORT STAFF I HAVE TAUGHT AND COACHED ON THE MSC IN MULTI-UNIT LEADERSHIP AND STRATEGY PROGRAMME OVER THE PAST SEVEN YEARS. THANK YOU FOR TESTING AND REFINING THE 75 MODELS IN THIS BOOK!

INTRODUCTION

Being an Area Manager in a retail service chain is both a fantastic and a frustrating experience. Leading and inspiring service teams to deliver their core purpose of ***generating memorable customer experiences*** is uplifting and energising. Achieving this objective in a complex and ambiguous space – in the middle of dispersed chains – can be debilitating! This book has been specifically written for aspirant and ambitious Area Managers, providing them with a series of models, frameworks and tools to help them overcome some of the challenges they face in order to thrive in their role and ***grow*** their businesses. But why is it aimed at this particular cohort and how will these models aid them?

Area Managers occupy a pivotal position in retail, hospitality and service-based chains. Responsible for two or more units of a similar format, they are expected to expedite the centre's policies and practices across their dispersed portfolio of stores to ensure consistency and uniformity. This isn't easy. Often, Area Managers are hampered by distance and the incommensurate demands of the centre and their units. Structural, functional and psychological distance between them, their stores and the centre hampers the day-to-day execution of their role: which is, namely, to achieve ***operational excellence*** and ***organic (like-for-like) growth*** without direct daily supervision. Irreconcilable objectives between the centre and their units also derail their role, with the centre favouring *efficiency* (based on a 'big picture view') and their units preferring *effectiveness* (due to their closeness to the customer).

A trinity of pressures bearing down upon the organisation (digitally, competitively and customer-related) also means that the Area Manager is often required to drive multiple changes through their portfolio at pace, with scant guidance or assistance from the centre. Compliance systems monitor the outcomes of these changes; threatening coercion and punishment if initiatives aren't 'landed' to time and specification. In actual fact, rather than acting as a facilitator for the Area Manager, the industrial systemisation of multi-unit enterprises brings added pressure through increased surveillance and 'measurement overload'. Couple these challenges with the fact that Area Managers might be operating a variety of units in different stages of the investment cycle, competing with other firms for scarce 'service-based' talent in local labour markets and facing hostile/agile local micro-market competition and one can understand why the role is so demanding!

In addition, Area Managers who have generally been promoted to this position from Unit or General Manager level have achieved advancement because of a high level of technical competence in *one* unit. However, managing a portfolio of units 'at a distance' requires an extended skill set, including more sophisticated behavioural and cognitive (thinking) capabilities. Sometimes, former Unit Managers – who try and manage each unit as if it were their own – will initially underperform against their peers and/or suffer from high levels of stress and burnout that result in them exiting the role. This book is aimed at preventing this problem and ameliorating some of the aforementioned issues that Area Managers face.

Aspirant and ambitious Area Managers want to succeed in the role: reward, recognition and, eventually, promotion to Retail Director level might follow! Their bosses and subordinates want them to be successful, because of their own reflected self-interest. This book provides a series of models and frameworks that can help Area Managers to expedite their job more effectively and **drive growth**. But why does it focus upon business frameworks, generally, and the models cited in the book in particular?

Models are extremely useful mechanisms. *First*, they convey problem-solving knowledge in a pictorial form and – as humans tend to think more figuratively and emotionally, rather than rationally – can be extremely effective vehicles for increasing levels of understanding and insight. Models are an antidote to ponderous, dry words and narrative which Area Managers have neither the time nor inclination to absorb. *Second*, they can be used – because of their integrated linkages and connections – as a practical analytical tool to enable managers to resolve issues and drive performance. *Third*, models help managers to look at challenges from a different perspective, affording them the opportunity to make greater sense of their context and role.

The models in this book have been selected *and adapted* on the basis that they add real value to an Area Manager's role and capacity to act effectively. Having written extensively about the subject of area management over the past six years and taught hundreds of Area Managers in both academic contexts and industry masterclasses, I have selected a range of concepts and models that have resonated with the recipients during face-to-face interactions. Some models in this book have been *adapted* from classic 'Harvard-type' frameworks, whilst most others are *my own creation* – based on area management research, feedback and observation (elucidated in my previous six books on multi-unit enterprises[1]). Some have been scientifically tested; others are proposed as useful prompts and checklists for aspirant or ambitious Area Managers. But how is the book structured in order to give optimal guidance to its principal readership?

Essentially, the book is structured around an integrated framework:

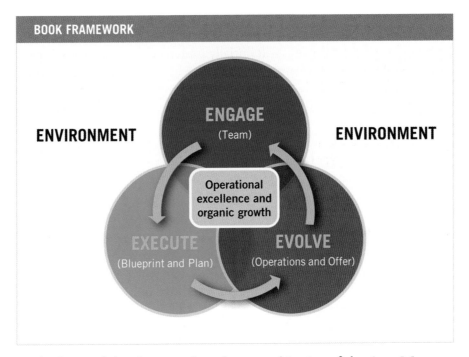

At the heart of this framework is the core objective of the Area Manager (AM): to achieve operational excellence and drive organic growth. These aims underpin all the models that feature in this book. There are five main elements, however, that enfold our understanding of the role and how performance can be optimised, and these form the basis of the main sections of the book:

Section 1 – Environment
Models in this section unpack the external and internal context in which an Area Manager operates. Here, models relating to strategic analysis, choice and implementation are intended to help the Area Manager **_understand_** their wider environment and its impact upon their role.

1 Edger, C. (2012) *Effective Multi-Unit Leadership – Local Leadership in Multi-Site Situations*, Farnham: Gower Business Publishing; (2013) *International Multi-Unit Leadership – Developing Local Leaders in Multi-Site Operations*, Farnham: Gower Business Publishing; (2014 & 2015) *Professional Area Management – Leading at a Distance in Multi-Unit Enterprises*, 1st and 2nd revised edition, Oxford: Libri; (2015) *Professional Area Management – Leading at a Distance in Multi-Unit Enterprises*, 2nd edition, Oxford: Libri; Edger, C., and Emmerson, A. (2015) *Franchising – How Both Sides Can Win*, Oxford: Libri; Edger, C., and Hughes, T. (2016) *Effective Brand Leadership – Be Different. Stay Different. Or Perish!* Oxford: Libri.

Section 2 – Engage

Having understood their environment, engaging ***their team*** is the first port of call for the Area Manager. They run a dispersed portfolio of B2C businesses requiring a high degree of emotional connectivity with customers, across multiple 'transaction touchpoints'. Their units' relative isolation and distance from the centre mean that Area Managers must work to establish a high level of rapport and 'buy-in' with their followers to achieve high levels of emotional contagion with the customer and superior levels of operational excellence in order to generate growth. Models in this section provide theoretical and practical insight into how Area Managers can more effectively engage with their followers.

Section 3 – Execute

Engagement will help facilitate the *execution* of the ***blueprint and the plan***. In this sense both 'engage' and 'execute' are not mutually exclusive – high levels of engagement will impact quality of execution. However, there are certain practices (both bureaucratic and ideological) that will enable the Area Manager to drive excellence and growth. Models in this section provide both a route map and analytical support to the Area Manager in pursuance of executing the brand and the plan.

Section 4 – Evolve

It is important that the AM has locked down executional hygiene factors before (s)he can seamlessly implement top-down change and/or evolve local ***operations and the offer***. Models in this section will deal with solutions relating to implementing top-down change and generating local innovation and creativity.

Section 5 – Personal Characteristics

What are the key personal attributes and skills AMs require to engage, execute and evolve service operations in complex and ambiguous MUE environments? This section will outline the five key personal characteristics of effective AMs, namely: emotional intelligence, expertise, entrepreneurism (connected to engage, execute and evolve respectively), energy and ethics.

Each section will deconstruct the relevant models by highlighting their *purpose* and core *principles/components*, followed by their principal *issues* and how the Area Manager can make *practical use* of the framework. I wish you every success in your journey through the models and sincerely hope that it adds serious value to your understanding of, and performance in, this fantastic role.

SECTION 1
ENVIRONMENTAL
Understanding

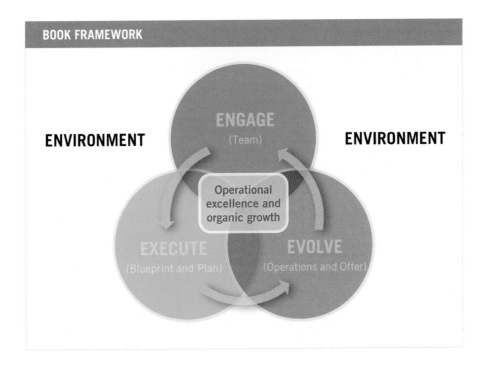

Effective Area Managers must understand the external and internal environment in which they operate in order to make sense of their role 'in context'. The environmental models in this section help the Area Manager to unpack both the competitive position and internal dynamics of their organisation and district.

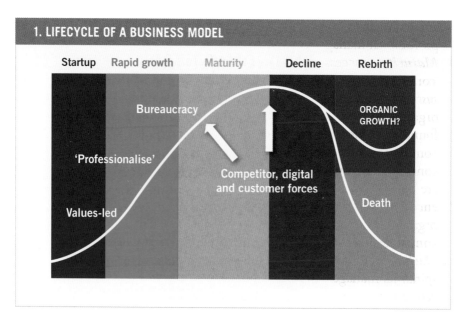

1. LIFECYCLE OF A BUSINESS MODEL

Startup   Rapid growth   Maturity   Decline   Rebirth

Bureaucracy

'Professionalise'

ORGANIC GROWTH?

Competitor, digital and customer forces

Death

Values-led

Purpose

The Lifecycle of a Business Model (LBM) provides a caricatured account of the life stages of a typical multi-unit service business. Starting with the founding stage – where the firm has a loose values-based culture – the LBM conceives of businesses as transitioning through a growth spurt until the point at which it professionalises its systems, thereafter entering a mature phase characterised by ossified inert bureaucracy driving the firm into decline, sparking either renewal or death in the latter stages. Intervening forces that impinge upon the organisation during its mature phase (digital, competitive or customer) are envisaged as accelerating a firm's descent towards death or rebirth.

Components/Principles

1. *Start-Up* – at this point the multi-unit firm has a 'big idea' and found a 'market place with a market space'. It has identified an unfulfilled customer need and establishes itself as an authentic organisation. At this stage – probably reliant on the energy and vision of the '*ORIGINATOR*' founder entrepreneur – the organisation is bound together by a strong values-based system ('the way we do things around here').

2. *Rapid Growth* – success breeds success! The multi-unit firm embarks on a major roll-out programme to reach out to customers and markets. During this phase, its rapid growth increases spans of managerial control and distance, threatening uniformity and consistence; behaviours cannot be controlled solely by values at this juncture. Rigorous systemisation is

applied (usually) through the recruitment of a cadre of *'ESCALATOR'* professional managers.

3. ***Maturity*** – success breeds failure! Professionalisation has tipped into a 'command and control' compliance approach – bureaucracy rules and *sustainer* managers struggle to maintain traction. Members of the organisation are beginning to lose sight of its original purpose and founding values. The firm – confronted by formidable forces (digital, competitor and demographic) – lacks the agility or imagination to continue its growth trajectory. At this point, *'EVOLVER'* leaders who are 'paranoid incrementalists' can fashion an upturn in fortunes through encouraging relentless innovation, but – more often than not – the organisation is stuck in a creative cul-de-sac, experiencing modest annual decline.

4. ***Decline*** – failure breeds failure! The firm is now into a potential death spiral. Its management can either acknowledge its precarious position, acting swiftly to reverse its parlous situation or face extinction.

5. ***Rebirth*** – failure breeds success! Existing or (more likely) new *'REVIVER'* management galvanises the organisation, recapturing its mojo by – in most instances – using a burning platform approach combined with a rediscovery of its true north which re-invigorates the firm with a renewed sense of purpose and direction.

6. ***Death*** – failure spirals into death! The firm's failure is irreversible either due to starvation (lack of financial resources to invest in a new direction), incompetence (managerial ineptitude) or obsolescence (a market no longer exists for its products and services). Time to call the administrators in…

Issues

- **Deterministic** – the LBM presupposes that singular firms transition through a series of sequential stages but some organisations (multi-branded chains for instance) will have elements of their portfolio that are 'running at different speeds'. Some brands within the portfolio might be in decline and are being milked before they expire in order to provide funds for brands that are in the stellar growth phase.

- **Timeframe** – the LBM does not reference time. In reality – depending on an organisation's sector/segment positioning – firms can transition through phases quicker than others (for instance technology companies can pass though the cycle more rapidly than hospitality organisations). Also, some disruptive forces (say economic or regulatory) can destroy what seem to be perfectly robust business models virtually overnight.

How AMs can use the Model

AMs can use this model to make sense of both their organisational and district lifecycle positioning, asking themselves the following questions:

– Where does my organisation/brand sit on the LBM? What are the consequences for my district?
– Where does my district sit on the LBM? Is it related to organisational factors or district-related issues? How do I continue my growth trajectory or reboot the district to find growth? (The consequences of not doing so ending in site disposals and/or closures!) Remember, have high expectations and aspirations – they will ultimately determine results and performance outcomes. Do not accept mediocrity!

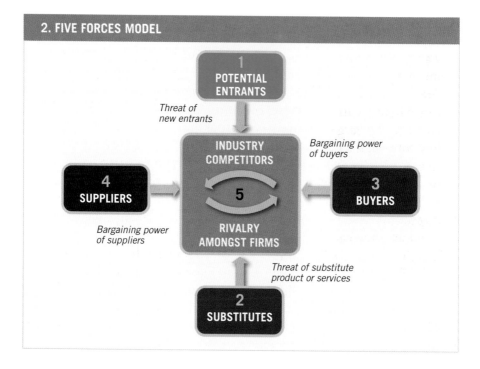

Purpose

Porter's[2] model isolates the five specific forces that determine the level of industry sales/margin *attractiveness* by focussing upon the threats posed by substitute products, established competitors, potential new entrants, suppliers and customers. An *unattractive* industry is one in which these

---

2 Adapted from Porter, M.E. (1985, 1998) *Competitive Advantage: Creating and Maintaining Performance*, The Free Press, a Division of Simon & Schuster Adult Publishing Company.

forces act to drive down average sales/margins. Porter argues that a good five forces analysis can suggest opportunities that companies can take advantage of to achieve above-average sales/margins.

Components/Principles

1. *Potential Entrants* – refers to new entrants which threaten the firm's livelihood within any given market. Management should therefore determine which levels/types of entry barriers are required to deter/repel new entrants such as: higher scale economies, higher levels of brand positioning/loyalty, higher levels of sunk capital, inimitable advantages (IP, tacit knowledge, machinery, technology, supply chain etc.), encouraging 'protective' regulation and 'entry deterring price' (low or high!).

2. *Substitutes* – refers to how easily a firm's product or service can be copied/cannibalised by substitute offers. Firms should be particularly wary of 'substitutional disrupters' who achieve a significant improvement in the price/performance trade off!

3. *Buyers* – refers to the extent to which customers of the product/service can bargain with the firm. Power for the buyer is increased if the customer is a large volume purchaser or buys in bulk during periods of low volume; is a purchaser of undifferentiated products (making it easy to play suppliers off against one another); and possesses large amounts of information about the firm's sales/margins (particularly if margins are low).

4. *Suppliers* – refers to organisations supplying an industry and the extent to which they can exert 'supplier power/influence' over firm sales and margins. Power for suppliers is at its greatest when there are a few selling to multiple buyers or when they have alternative customer/channel choices and they can cut out layers within the supply chain by 'integrating forwards' by producing/selling direct to a firm's customers.

5. *Competitive Rivalry* – refers to existing competitors and the advantages they might possess that could disrupt a firm's competitive position. Dangers from rival competition is increased if there are multiple competitors who are equally strong; industry growth is anaemic meaning that competitors focus upon 'dividing' rather than 'expanding' the market; the sector/industry (such as multi-unit retail) has high fixed costs which drives capacity-filling behaviours; products/services are commoditised forcing competitors to race to the bottom on price; there is strategic diversity amongst competitors making it difficult to predict future behaviour; and if there are high exit barriers due to economic or legal circumstances.

Issues

- **Confined to Industry Level** – Porter conceived of his model as an economic tool for analysing macro industry structures, helping managers to improve their strategic decision-making capability. Its problem is that it doesn't address hierarchies of sectors, competitive clusters or markets. The reality is that the average company competes in multiple industries (lines of business), yet this model does not reflect that complexity. Additionally, explaining firm performance through industry structure has subsequently been challenged on the basis that it only explains 10% of a firm's performance variance: a company will not be successful merely because it operates in an attractive industry (other factors more powerfully explain firm performance).
- **Static** – the five forces model only addresses the here and now, and can thus be accused of being static and short-termist. Also, whilst it is a good framework for analysis, it fails to take into account matters relating to implementation.

How AMs can use the Model

In spite of these issues, Area Managers can use Porter's model – as it was originally intended – as a brainstorming device to help members of their team to understand their organisation's competitive position. It provides a useful starting point to generate debate and discussion, enabling managers to make sense of their broad competitive environment. AMs would do well to remember Porter's dictum that companies that wish to achieve sustainable competitive advantage 'learn faster' and 'execute better' than their competitors!

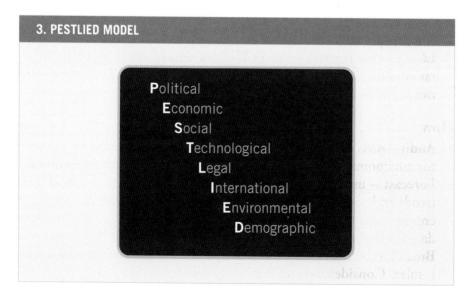

3. PESTLIED MODEL

Political
Economic
Social
Technological
Legal
International
Environmental
Demographic

Purpose

The PESTLIED Model provides a mnemonic checklist of the various macro-environmental factors that managers need to consider when analysing the competitive position of an organisation.

Components/Principles

1. *Political* – local/regional/national government actions
2. *Economic* – fiscal policies (taxes and financial regulations)
3. *Social* – cultural norms, customs and trends and their predisposition to the firm/product
4. *Technological* – 'push' or 'pull' advances which effect product/service demand
5. *Legal* – 'enabling' or 'restrictive' legislation in relation to the sector/industry
6. *International* – exchange rates, currency fluctuations and cost of goods
7. *Environmental* – corporate social responsibility costs and requirements
8. *Demographic* – external labour market strength and population characteristics (age, wealth, education etc.)

Issues

- **Relative Importance** – this model provides a sequential checklist, but the relative importance of the PESTLIED factors will be ranked differently according to organisational positioning/industry.
- **Neglects Competition** – the model is silent in relation to competitors and how they are reacting/coping with these environmental factors. Hence, PESETLIED is best used in conjunction with the SWOT Analysis tool (see below) which combines an analysis of the firm, its competition and their environmental context.
- **Limited Application** – PESTLIED is often used to assess a current rather than future state because of the difficulty of forecasting macro-trends.

How AMs can use the Model

- **Audit** – AMs can use this checklist with their teams to analyse and audit the environmental position of their organisation/district.
- **Forecast** – used creatively, PESTLIED can be used to forecast future trends and scenario plan, acting as a kind of risk and resilience tool to ensure the AM's district has accounted for near and present dangers/opportunities.
- **Break Insularity** – AMs can use this model to make their teams less insular. Considering the impact that wider forces will have on the

organisation/district will increase levels of insight/maturity regarding the bounded constraints facing the policy makers within their businesses.

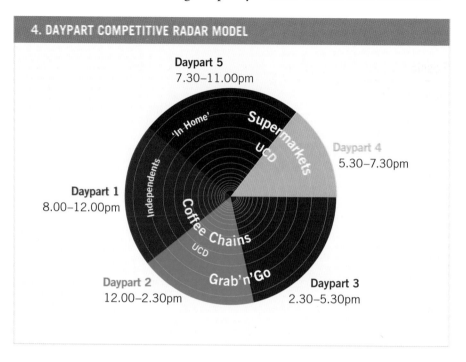

Purpose

The Daypart Competitive Radar Model[3] (DCRM) is a tool that can be used for analytical and discussion purposes to highlight where MUE (Multi-Unit Enterprise) businesses' main competitive threats/opportunities can be located at different times of the day. It can help managers understand the nature of their competition from a temporal perspective in order to help them adapt their products/services in a hybridised form throughout the main day/night-part sessions in order satisfy various consumer occasions; thereby optimising expensive land-based asset use.

Components/Principles

The DCRM envisages the organisation as being at the epicentre of an imaginary radar screen with local competitors ranging 'near' or 'far' (i.e. being highly or mildly threatening) in proximal terms during different dayparts. The DCRM highlighted above is an illustration of the competitive

3 Adapted from Wilson, S. (2013) Strategy and Branding Module, MSc Multi-Unit Leadership and Strategy Programme, Birmingham City University.

threats faced by a UK pub restaurant operation which has five daypart sessions with a variety of competitor (direct and substitute) offers that loom large at different sessions/occasions. (Note that this model takes it as read that the operation is in direct competition with other pub restaurant chains!)

Session Time	Occasion	Competition
8.00–12.00	Breakfast & Snacking	Independents and Coffee Chains
12.00–12.30	Lunch	UCD, Grab & Go and Coffee Chains
2.30–5.30	Snacking & Treats	Grab & Go and Coffee Chains
5.30–7.30	Family Dining	UCD, Supermarkets & In home
7.30–11.00	Dinner & Drinks (Socialising & Celebrating)	UCD, Supermarkets & In home

Issues

- **Different Days/Seasons** – one of the principal issues with this model is that businesses experience different competitive threats on *different days* and *different dayparts* due to intervening variables such as customer habit, weather, paydays, promotional pushes, seasonal changes, calendar events etc. This is a static model which can only be applied *generally* rather than specifically.
- **Accurate Estimation of Threat** – data on competitors (their trading patterns, item sales and profit) will be imperfect and is more likely to be qualitative observation rather than quantitative hard information. Managers must be extremely diligent in checking out their principal competition on a regular basis, and at different times on different days, to assess levels of competitive threat.
- **Destructive Opportunism** – care must be taken by operators that whilst they opportunistically cover dayparts they do not engage in non-value-added 'product creep' – i.e. products and services being randomly 'loaded' into the operation, increasing cost and derailing consistency and quality.

How AMs can use the Model

The DCRM can be used at a macro company level or a micro local market level. AMs can get their teams to do a DCRM to illustrate the local competitive offers who represent the greatest competitive threat during their main trading segments. It is suggested that AMs get their GMs to do

DCRMs for their units to reflect weekly rhythms (weekdays and weekends) and by season (key events and weather) when consumption and occasionality patterns will vary. Having got their GMs to do illustrative DCRMs, AMs can pose the following inter-related questions:

- Why are potential customers using alternative outlets at these times?
- What do we need to do to attract them? What types of resources/offer do we require to make this happen?
- How do we increase our penetration/usage during these different dayparts?
- How do we smooth out peaks and troughs?
- What do we need to stop, start and continue doing to attract customers?

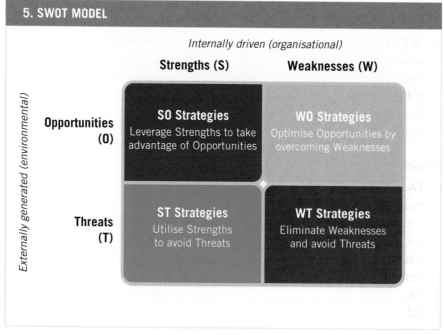

Purpose
The SWOT Model can be used to determine the competitive positioning of an organisation, enabling managers to match resources and responses to their external environment.

Principles and Components
This model juxtaposes internally derived organisational attributes (strengths and weaknesses) against external market forces (posing opportunities and threats):

1. *Strengths* – these are 'positive' internal attributes (i.e. branding, people, cash flow etc.)
2. *Weaknesses* – these will include negative internal characteristics (i.e. poor machinery, technology, facilities, product/market mix, gaps in capability etc.)
3. *Opportunities* – organic growth opportunities caused by market gaps opening up due to changing consumer needs, demographic changes etc.
4. *Threats* – these are external market threats to growth (i.e. macro-economic policy, new technology, legislation etc.)

The strategies that managers can deploy given the juxtaposition of forces are as follows:
1. *SO & ST Strategies* – these are fairly straightforward: the organisation should 'stick to the knitting' and concentrate what it is good at, avoiding activity for which it lacks capability
2. *WO Strategies* – this approach has more risk attached: the organisation must develop and/or acquire the requisite capabilities to 'outmuscle' its competitive set
3. *ST Strategies* – these involve so-called 'buy or bust' strategy pathways: here, managers might engage in expensive price cutting strategies to 'buy' market share!

Issues

- **Data Quality** – the degree to which managers can make informed judgements about their competitive position and preferred strategic response is contingent upon the quality of data at their disposal. Are their perceptions regarding their strengths (relative to those of the competition) realistic or delusional? Have they conducted a proper benchmarking exercise? Often managers will over-estimate their own firms' capabilities relative to their competitors, due to imprecise information or guided bias.
- **Analytical Strength** – the analytical utility of this model is rather thin unless it is combined with other models such as PESTLIED and Ansoff's Paths to Growth models.

How AMs can use this Model

AMs can use the SWOT framework to ask the following questions:
- Strengths – what do we (the organisation and/or my district) do well? What are our standout core competencies relative to our competition? (New recruits from competitors will provide excellent insights on both strengths and weaknesses.)

- Weaknesses – what are we lacking in? In which respects do we fall short in relation to our competitors?
- Opportunities – what enabling demographic, legislative or technological changes are taking place that we can exploit?
- Threats – what dangers do we face from changes in regulations and/or threats from substitute products that might threaten sales and dilute margins?

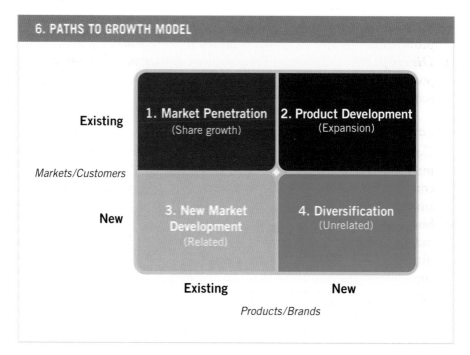

6. PATHS TO GROWTH MODEL

	Existing	New
Existing	**1. Market Penetration** (Share growth)	**2. Product Development** (Expansion)
New	**3. New Market Development** (Related)	**4. Diversification** (Unrelated)

Markets/Customers

Products/Brands

Purpose

Ansoff's[4] Paths to Growth Model enables managers to review, test, recommend and choose various growth strategies in light of the organisation's idiosyncratic product and market positioning. Its main premise is that *new* products and markets require differentiated growth strategies from *existing* products and markets.

Components/Principles

The main components of the model suggest that expansion-minded management should consider the following growth strategies:

1. ***Market Penetration*** – resources should be targeted at increasing market/customer share in *existing* markets (the so-called '*share growth*'

---

4 Adapted from Ansoff, I. (1968) *Corporate Strategy*, Penguin Publishing.

approach). This pathway to growth encourages managers to consider how they can pursue protect/build/consolidate (i.e. M&A) strategies.

2. ***Product Development*** – new products should be *expanded* into *existing* markets by using or acquiring new competencies/skills for the organisation.

3. ***New Market Development*** – managerial effort should be directed at expanding *new* markets for *existing* products. To this extent management should focus upon opening/harvesting new segments, channels, users and territories for *related* products by adopting enhanced marketing/promotional approaches (such as digital multi-media).

4. ***Diversification*** – new products (which are *unrelated* to the current portfolio) are developed/acquired through NPD, M&A or skills acquisition to attack *new* markets.

Issues

- **Competition** – the model fails to overlay competitor activities/intentions. To this extent managers should actively consider the competitive risks associated with pursuing any of the aforementioned strategies for market growth.

- **Simplicity** – the model presents four paths to growth in a manner that makes them seem mutually exclusive, a simple choice between four different options. In reality, firms often pursue multiple paths simultaneously, although their resource allocation will (or should) rationally favour paths which offer the greatest relative or absolute scale of opportunity.

How AMs can use the Model

AMs can use this model with their teams to discuss how they can fit existing/new products with existing/new markets and customers. Its emphasis upon growth means that at the very least it serves as a stimulant for discussion around growing sales. Questions that AMs can pose to their teams, in the context of using this model, might include:

- Market Penetration – how do we keep, nurture and defend our *existing* local market share with our *existing* product portfolio?

- Product Development – what *new* products/services can we develop to grow revenue streams from *existing* customers?

- New Market Development – how do we attract *new* customers with *existing* products through relaunch or repositioning interventions such as enhanced marketing activities (i.e. social media and digital)?

- Diversification – how do we use our current resources to launch/develop *new* products and services to attract *new* customers?

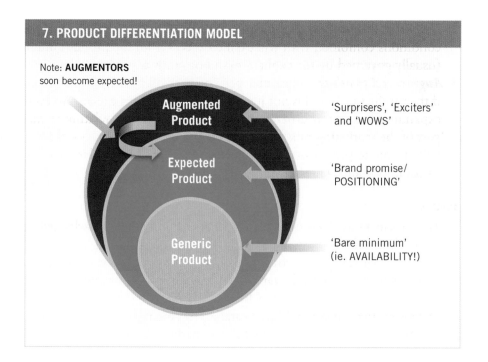

7. PRODUCT DIFFERENTIATION MODEL

Note: **AUGMENTORS** soon become expected!

- Augmented Product — 'Surprisers', 'Exciters' and 'WOWS'
- Expected Product — 'Brand promise/POSITIONING'
- Generic Product — 'Bare minimum' (ie. AVAILABILITY!)

Purpose

The Product Differentiation Model (PDM) is adapted from Theodore Levitt's seminal article[5] which makes the empirical observation that there is no such thing as a commodity product, because all goods and services can be differentiated through tangible and intangible means. Levitt's three-step product hierarchy (generic, expected and augmented) still resonates today as a route map that branded organisations should pursue to differentiate their offers. It should be noted that his fourth dimension – potential product – is excluded from the model above, for the simple reason that Ansoff's Paths to Growth Model (see previous model) deals more specifically with factors relating to related and unrelated product diversification.

Components/Principles

According to Levitt, a product consists of a 'range of possibilities':

1. *Generic Product* – this is the substantive, rudimentary, substantive 'thing' about the product (such as food being available in a food service outlet). On its own, it has low 'sales relator' properties and is merely a passport to play in the market.

---

4 Adapted from Levitt, T. (1980) 'Marketing Success through Differentiation – of Anything', *Harvard Business Review*, January–February.

2. ***Expected Product*** – these include the customer's minimum purchase conditions combined with what (s)he expects from the product/brand (usually governed by the explicit 'brand or product promise').

3. ***Augmented Product*** – customer perceptions will outstrip expectations if the product or brand is not just limited to what they expect. An ever-expanding 'bundle of differentiating value satisfaction' relating to any part of the marketing mix (place, goods, price, promotions, people etc.) will stimulate propensity to purchase, repeat business, advocacy and (most importantly) new customers.

Issues

- **Transition Time** – a problem with the model (readily acknowledged by Levitt himself) is that Augmenters become subsumed within the Expected category by consumers over time. However, temporal dependencies are glossed over by the model, with a presumption that their perception as 'added value' by consumers will depend on the length of time as 'first movers' within a category/segment.

- **Product Focus** – Levitt's model has an unashamed product rather than a services-based focus although it does make forceful distinctions between 'hard' tangible (functional) and 'soft' intangible (emotional) dimensions of the product hierarchy.

How AMs can use the Model

Using the model AMs can review the following questions with their teams:

- Generic – what are the basic 'must have' hygiene factors of our product/brand? What are the base 'pay to play' elements of our offer?
- Expected – what do customer expect from our product/brand (based on its essential positioning/promise)? Is this being delivered? Which Augmenters (previously viewed as proprietary differentiators) have now been absorbed into this 'expected' category?
- Augmenters – what aspects of our product are differentiated from the competition? How do we build clear PODs (points of difference) that are *low cost* to us but are of *high perceived value* to the customer?

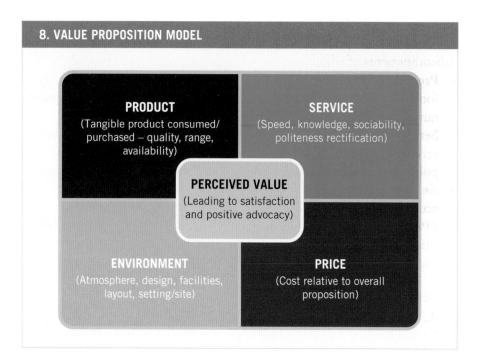

8. VALUE PROPOSITION MODEL

PRODUCT
(Tangible product consumed/
purchased – quality, range,
availability)

SERVICE
(Speed, knowledge, sociability,
politeness rectification)

PERCEIVED VALUE
(Leading to satisfaction
and positive advocacy)

ENVIRONMENT
(Atmosphere, design, facilities,
layout, setting/site)

PRICE
(Cost relative to overall
proposition)

Purpose

The Value Proposition Model illustrates the four main 'experiential' attributes of a retail business that require balanced alignment to achieve positive customer advocacy and commercial success; whatever the differentiated positioning of the brand (in premium, mid or discount-led segments of the market). Its central argument is that once all the main cornerstones of the brand are in place, it is the way that they are kept within relative balance with one another that is a main determinant of success or failure.

Components/Principles

The VPM is based upon an equation:

$$PA = CSftPVft(£p,p,e,s)$$

PA (Positive Advocacy) is an outcome of CS (Customer Satisfaction)
which is a ft (function) of PV (Perceived Value)
which is a ft (function) of £p (price), p (product), e (environment) and s (service).

The central premise of this equation is that positive advocacy by existing customers (by both word-of-mouth and 'mouse') results from high levels of customer satisfaction derived from high levels of perceived value (conscious and unconscious feelings of a 'good deal') derived from an experiential combination of price, product, environment and service, the main subcomponents of which are:

- **Product** – this encompasses the tangible served product (for instance, food and beverages in food service) including aspects such as quality, range, availability etc.
- **Service** – including 'appropriate' speed during all aspects of the chain of service (so-called 'touches'), combined with sociability, knowledge, politeness and the ability to immediately resolve/rectify breakdowns
- **Environment** – factors include the actual site (location and accessibility), design, facilities, layout and atmosphere
- **£Price** – incorporating the 'unbundled' or 'bundled' experience in which price should be relative to other VPM factors such as product, service and environmental quality.

Issues

- **Analytical Linkages** – most organisations have customer satisfaction insight (such as Net Promoter Score and digital analysis) and a plethora of financial data but fail to make appropriate 'what' and 'why' linkages.
- **Perceived Value** – customers use a brand with pre-set expectations, but establishing what these are and how they should be met/bettered is problematic. Often there will be mismatches between what operators believe customers want and what they *truly* value.

How AMs can use this Model

At either a district or a unit level, take the customer data (company driven or spontaneous outputs from other sources such as social media, message boards etc.) and use the VPM as an anchor for the following inter-related questions:

- What matters most to my customers (don't just look at what they say – look at how they act!)? What distinctive benefits do we currently offer to satisfy their needs, desires, aspirations and feelings?
- Is there any evidence of the 'deadly combination' effect at play; for instance, where customers feel that current levels of service or environmental quality do not justify the price?
- What elements are degrading the current 'experiential equation'? What are the current 'break/sensitivity points'? How can they be fixed? How can I eliminate costs of service that don't matter and finance the ones that do!
- What immediate controllables (EMOTIONAL service being the obvious lever) can we drive to impact impressions of perceived value

and, consequently, rates of customer satisfaction? How do we ensure customer perceptions exceed expectations leading to high levels of attraction, loyalty and advocacy?

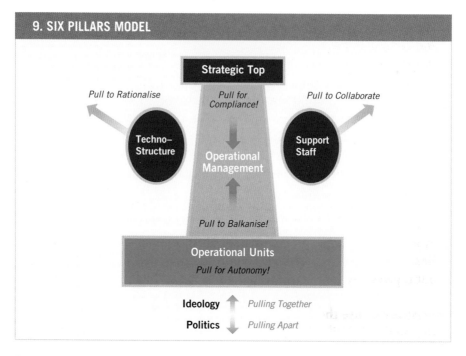

9. SIX PILLARS MODEL

Purpose

The Six Pillars Model is adapted from Mintzberg's[6] classic structural illustration of the 'common' organisational form, assisting our understanding as to where 'tensions' and pulls within the 'typical' firm exist. Greater insight into these persistent tensions between the various structural components of the firm aids greater managerial 'sense making' of co-ordination/alignment issues and their potential solutions.

Components/Principles

Mintzberg's proposition is that most organisations incorporate six fundamental building blocks: strategic management, middle management (reworked as operational management in this model), the technostructure, support staff, operational core (operational units in this framework) and the ideological component. The tensions/pulls in the model show where co-ordination issues might lie, and caricature behaviours including:

6 Mintzberg, H. (1992) *Structure in Fives – Designing Effective Organizations*, 2nd edition, Upper Saddle River, NJ: Pearson Education Inc.

1. ***Strategic Top*** – 'Pull for Compliance': preference for central *efficiency*, order, outcome certainty and homogeneity
2. ***Operational Management*** – 'Pull to Balkanise': preference for local *effectiveness*, autonomy and *heterogeneity*
3. ***Techno-structure*** – 'Pull to Rationalise': preference for 'one size fits all' and consistency across the firm
4. ***Support Staff*** – 'Pull to Collaborate': preference for cupertino behaviours in order to get 'the basics' completed
5. ***Operating Units*** – 'Pull for Autonomy': preference for 'local fit' and agility
6. ***Ideology*** – 'Pulling Together': preference for aligned values and a healthy culture (which can be undermined by 'pulling apart' politics).

Issues

- **Generalisability** – this model can be criticised for its universality: clearly, different firms due to history, leadership capability and situation will experience different types of tensions.
- **Basis for Action?** – the Six Pillars model points out potential tensions but it gives few clues as to how they might be resolved!

How AMs can use the Model

Analysing the six building blocks within the organisation by turn, get your team to address the following questions:

- Where does power lie within the organisation? (Usually, with the building block which exerts the dominant 'pull' on co-ordination.) What are the implications for us as a team? How do we harness this power for our own benefit?
- To what extent does the ideology of the organisation 'hold things together'? What values could you as a team agree upon and adhere to, in order to optimise performance?

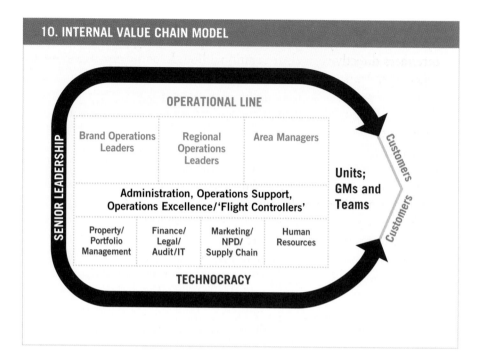

Purpose

The Internal Value Chain Model (IVCM) illustrates the interlocking functions within a typical MUE (Multi-Unit Enterprise). Its main purpose is to highlight how internal processes prop up and feed into the operational line and how all operational/corporate functions should be aligned behind the main point of direct customer interface: namely, the units populated by GMs and their service-providing teams.

Components and Principles

The model has six main elements:

1. **Strategic Leadership** – these *strategic decision makers* are responsible for the strategic direction of the firm, macro-resource allocation and external stakeholder management. As the arrows on the IVCM indicate, successful businesses are generally those in which strategic leaders are 'in' the business – reaching down and touching/feeling the pulse of the frontline – rather than merely sitting 'on' the business in a detached, dispassionate and disengaged manner. in a detached, dispassionate and disengaged manner.

2. **Technocracy** – these *resource holders and policy makers* are populated by 'expert' functionaries covering key activities such as property/maintenance, finance/legal/audit and IT, marketing/new product development/supply chain and HR/talent management.

3. ***Administration and Support*** – these *enabling support services* provided by the technocracy are often bundled up into a 'support centre' which interfaces directly with the operational line. In some organisations, so-called operational excellence personnel (experts in operational efficiency and effectiveness) and designated 'flight controllers' who regulate the flow of information/communication/initiatives to the line will also sit between the technocracy and operations.

4. ***Operational Line*** – typically seen as *implementers*, this cohort is populated by strategic brand operations leaders, 'interfacing' regional operations leaders and 'local' Area Managers who manage districts of between 8 and 30 units (depending on business type and sector).

5. ***Units and Service Providers*** – these *customer-facing personnel* are the most important link in the chain as the GM, his/her unit management/supervisory team and service providers are the main point of impact with the customer. In short, they are the face of the company. The degree to which the preceding pieces of the jigsaw fit together in order to support this cohort will be a major determinant of customer delight or dismay! Ultimately, the internal service provided to this frontline population will have a major impact on external/customer perceptions of service.

Issues

- **Intangibles** – the model is normative and descriptive: concentrating on tangible issues of structural alignment/congruence. It does not deal with intangible issues such as competence, power, ideology, politics and culture; all important elements that contribute to either success/failure within MUEs.

- **Efficiency vs Effectiveness** – in reality whilst strategic leaders and technocrats will have a preference for efficiency ('doing it right'), the operational line will (due to their closeness to customers) lean towards effectiveness ('doing the right thing'). This tension is not highlighted by this model. In order to increase effectiveness in MUEs, it is highly advisable that strategic leaders 'get the functions' as close to the operational line as possible by 'implanting' marketeers and HR in the regional operational line.

How AM can use this Model

– Context – the IVCM helps AMs understand their position within the value chain

– Sensemaking – it highlights for AMs how all the interlocking parts of the value chain fit together

– Customer facing – the IVCM will help augment an understanding amongst AMs and their teams concerning the criticality of their customer-facing position.

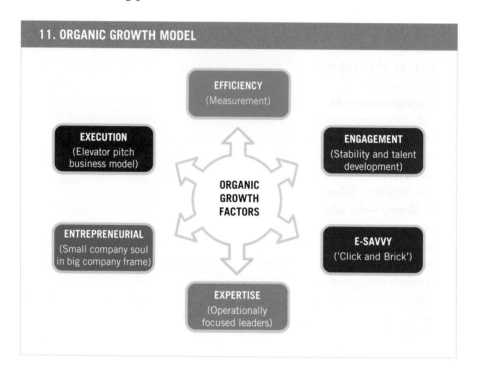

11. ORGANIC GROWTH MODEL

EFFICIENCY
(Measurement)

EXECUTION
(Elevator pitch business model)

ENGAGEMENT
(Stability and talent development)

ORGANIC GROWTH FACTORS

ENTREPRENEURIAL
(Small company soul in big company frame)

E-SAVVY
('Click and Brick')

EXPERTISE
(Operationally focused leaders)

Purpose

Derived from over 100 case studies I have drawn from MUEs, the Organic Growth Model (OGM) highlights the six interconnected drivers of organisational organic growth (like-for-like un-invested sales growth). As such, it illustrates company-level cornerstones of organic growth which – as a key indicator of underlying company health – are an important element of long-term corporate sustainability, as opposed to tactical landgrab M&A or price-led sales gorging.

Components and Principles

The six E's of organic growth in the OGM include:

1. *Execution* – in dispersed multi-unit contexts, organic growth firms are great at executing the basics day-in-day out. This is partially due to the fact that they have (in US parlance) *elevator-pitch* business models that are simple to understand, well documented and easily grasped by all internal stakeholders. A by-product of this simplicity is the (relative) ease

by which they can implement and 'land things' quickly in a diffuse multi-site context in order to counter competitive threats and/or create competitive advantage.

2. ***Efficiency*** – strong like-for-like companies are vigilant/diligent with regards to cost control measurement/monitoring (COGs, labour, wastage, shrinkage and OMCs). They have a grip upon the business *but* not at the expense of destroying engagement or entrepreneurial behaviours!

3. ***Engagement*** – in parallel with the point above, execution/efficiency is aided through *authentic* – rather than rhetoric-based – HRM systems (talent development, recognition, two-way communication and remuneration). Great HRM leads to higher engagement: better satisfaction, lower turnover/absenteeism, higher stability, more discretionary effort etc.

4. ***E-Savvy*** – in addition to the above, companies with high levels of organic growth are e-savvy: that is to say, they are adopters of new 'push' and 'pull' technologies that create value within their businesses. Using new technologies to drive customer awareness, traffic and throughputs is taken as a given by these organisations.

5. ***Expertise*** – these inter-linked features are aided by the fact that the senior leadership cadres are knowledgeable and operationally focussed. Understanding the nuts and bolts of the business enables them to take well-informed decisions that accelerate the growth trajectory of the business. Great leaders are 'in' rather than 'on' the business.

6. ***Entrepreneurism*** – another feature of firms that enjoy sustained organic growth is their company-wide obsession with invention and continuous improvement with regards to product and service delivery. By adopting a small company mindset within a large company frame, these firms constantly ask themselves 'what should we stop, start or continue doing?' to improve the customer offer during all trading dayparts!

Issues

- **Interconnectedness** – dependencies between each construct within the OGM are not fully tested and understood.
- **Relative Weighting** – in some industries/organisations some components of the model will be more influential than others.

How AMs can use the Model

AMs can use the OGM with their teams to make sense of their organisational environment, facilitating an understanding of the mechanisms which enable/degrade organic growth. At a district level, AMs can use it as a soft analytical tool, posing the following questions:

- Execution – do you understand the *what* and *how* of the blueprint?
- Efficiency – do you understand the key input/output metrics and KPIs?
- Engagement – are your people sufficiently psychologically attached and motivated?
- E-Savvy – are we leveraging digital *pull* (social media) and *push* (in-house enabling technology) to drive sales?
- Expertise – does our team have the requisite levels of explicit (codified and articulated) and tacit (uncodified and unarticulated) skill to drive growth
- Entrepreneurism – are we constantly seeking ways to incrementally improve our businesses (its marketing mix and proposition)?

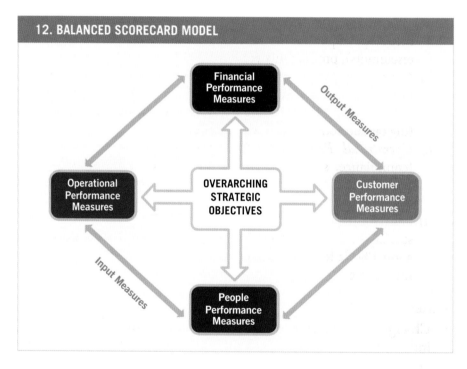

Purpose

Devised by Kaplan and Norton[7], the Balanced Scorecard Model (BSC) is a framework for defining *input* and *output* objectives of an organisation which can then be cascaded down the firm. It is cognisant of the fact that intertwined financial and customer *outputs* are the result (most prominently within MUEs) of operational and people *input* drivers. Today, the scorecard has

---

7 Adapted from Kaplan, R., and Norton, D. (1996) *The Balanced Scorecard: Translating Strategy into Action*, Cambridge, MA: Harvard Business School Press.

morphed into 'dashboard' and 'traffic light' indicators in many organisations.

Components and Principles

1. *Overall Strategic Objectives* – companies should begin by defining their top-level strategic objectives by addressing questions such as: what business are we in? what are we trying to achieve? and how are we going to get there? The BSC which backs up this strategy is essentially a tactical instrument that measures progress towards superordinate objectives, being set (generally) on an annual basis and regularly reviewed/scrutinised (weekly, monthly and quarterly).

2. *BSC Elements*
   a) *Financial Performance Measures* (Outputs) – these generally include sales, margin, profit, ROI, ROCE, EVA, stock turn, sales per square metre, spend per head, items sold (cover turns or number of meals in restaurants), product mix etc.
   b) *Customer Performance Measures* (Outputs) – these generally include NPS, customer and stakeholder satisfaction indicators, complaints 'per cheque', retention, frequency, market share, 'word of mouse' (digital and social media), dwell times etc.
   c) *Operational Performance Measures* (Inputs) – internal quality (compliance, standards, health & hygiene), availability, time to market, new sales % of overall sales, internal process efficiency, supply chain resilience etc.
   d) People Performance Measures (Inputs) – employee satisfaction, stability/retention, turnover, grievances/disciplinaries, skills/capability audit (% fit for needs), succession pipeline, learning and growth metrics etc.

Issues

- **Change** – as strategy imperceptibly morphs over time, scorecard indicators need changing/melding; something that organisations are notoriously bad at doing!
- **Dependencies** – policy makers must ensure that they have conducted an analytical process that confirms a high level of dependency (linkages/connections) between the various input/output measures; again, this is poorly done in most organisations.
- **Less is More** – organisations must concentrate on a limited number of key drivers for the purposes of clarity; unfortunately, many organisations overcomplicate things by putting in place too many KPIs 'to cover all the ground'.
- **Cascade** – these measures must be articulated, cascaded and incentivised

at all levels within the organisation to ensure congruity and the alignment of resources/effort for optimal outcomes; sometimes organisations fail to articulate BSC measures all the way down the chain, rendering them optimistic 'wish lists'.

How AMs can use this Model

Most organisations will take a balanced scorecard approach (although most will inevitably weight incentives to financial outputs). AMs should:
- Pay particular attention to the input drivers (operations and people); these will move outputs in the right direction
- Ensure objectives are cascaded to 'micro' levels (i.e. service provider) within their portfolios (through shift/session KPIs)
- Prioritise particular indicators in certain units at certain times
- Explain the various dependencies to their team so that so that they can 'read' the scorecard/dashboard!

13. OPERATIONS MULTI-LAYERED NET MODEL

Store Managers	District Managers	Regional Vice-Presidents	Divisional Heads
		Strategy/policy refinement	
	Strategy/policy implementation		
		Strategy/policy compliance and alignment	
	Competitive market intelligence and positioning		
Task execution			
Task/tactics compliance			
Local problem solving			
	System problem solving		
Fixing of performance problems			
Coaching and development of managers and employees			

Purpose

Garvin and Levesque's[8] Operations Multi-Layered Net Model (MLNM) is the result of extensive empirical research into optimal operational line performance within MUEs (Multi-Unit Enterprises). The model illustrates how best-practice MUEs co-ordinate operating activities through deploying

8 Adapted from Garvin, D., and Levesque, L. (2008) 'The Multi-Unit Enterprise', *Harvard Business Review*, June, pp.1–11.

a multi-layered net of overlapping accountabilities through the operational line to prevent slippage. Most significantly, eight out of the ten accountabilities fall within the domain of the Area Manager – more than any other line role in the MUE. Locating these eight key accountabilities from the MLNM affords MUEs and their AMs greater insight into the key requirements for the role.

Components/Principles

The MLNM sub-divides the line into four tiers: store managers, district (area) managers, regional VPs and divisional heads. The eight key overlapping accountabilities for AMs, and how AMs should expedite them, are as follows:

1. *Strategy/Policy Implementation* – AMs to ensure seamless policy execution 'on the ground'
2. *Competitive/Market Intelligence* – AMs act as conduits for local insights/trend information in a 'middle-up-down' fashion
3. *Task Execution* – AMs ensure tasks are fulfilled for operational excellence purposes
4. *Task/Tactics Compliance* – AMs facilitate quick tactical implementation
5. *Local Problem Solving* – AMs fulfil a local 'troubleshooting'/'fixer' role
6. *Systemic Problem Solving* – AMs fulfil an analytical 'operational solutions' role
7. *Fixing of Performance Problems* – AMs work with their store managers and teams to resolve performance issues
8. *Coaching and Development of Managers/Employees* – AMs fulfil a 'local HRM' role.

The traps that Garvin and Levesque advise Area Managers to avoid include failing to build effective store management teams, overemphasising compliance by focusing solely upon audits, relying too heavily on direction/control (not enough on coaching) and imposing a single management style.

Issues

- **Prioritisation** – the model lists accountabilities hierarchically rather than in order of AM priority. Also, although Garvin and Levesque emphasise that HRM is one of the most important roles of the AM, this isn't made evident by this model.
- **Skills Requirement** – Garvin and Levesque hint at the skills required by AMs to fulfil these accountabilities, but fail to provide a comprehensive account of the competencies required to expedite the role successfully.

How AMs can use this Model

AMs can make sense of their current role by checking what they do against an empirical framework which describes what they *should* do. New or aspirant AMs can see what additional responsibilities they will have to assume if they are promoted into the role from store manager (i.e. strategy/policy implementation, competitive/market intelligence and systemic problem solving). New AMs should note that most of these additional activities are *cognitive* (thinking) rather than behavioural and/or technically based skills.

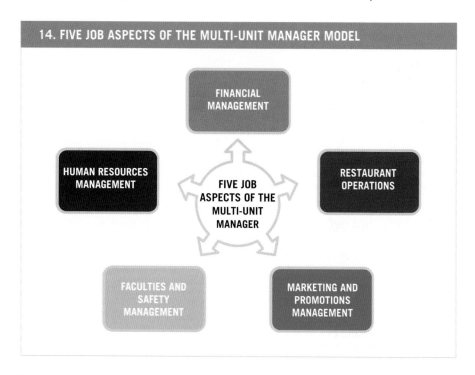

14. FIVE JOB ASPECTS OF THE MULTI-UNIT MANAGER MODEL

FINANCIAL MANAGEMENT

HUMAN RESOURCES MANAGEMENT

FIVE JOB ASPECTS OF THE MULTI-UNIT MANAGER

RESTAURANT OPERATIONS

FACULTIES AND SAFETY MANAGEMENT

MARKETING AND PROMOTIONS MANAGEMENT

Purpose

Umbreit's[9] inductive research into the main functions of the multi-unit manager (Area Manager) in US food service was the first major attempt to measure and categorise what AMs do. His analysis produced a framework containing five major job aspects which – after considerable empirical enquiry – has been ranked by successive academics in order of priority (with Operations and HRM usually ranked #1 or #2). This framework has been plagiarised, adapted and tested many times since, and still remains relevant to the AM role today!

---

9 Adapted from Umbreit, W.T. (1989) 'Multi-Unit Management: Managing at a Distance', *Cornell Hotel and Restaurant Administration Quarterly*, 30(1), pp.52–9.

Components and Principles

Umbreit's five AM job aspects – ranked in order of priority (according to most research) – are as follows:

1. *Restaurant Operations* – enforces consistent company standards, systems and procedures; evaluates product quality; implements new systems; oversees the delivery of positive customer service; supervises new product introductions; and monitors unit-management activities
2. *Human Resources Management* – supervises effective orientation, training and management of employees; teaches unit managers how to manage people; provides quality feedback; and develops promotable managers
3. *Financial Management* – maintains profitability of units by monitoring performance, preparing budgets, developing forecasts, authorising expenditures, controlling costs and reviewing results with unit managers
4. *Marketing and Promotions Management* – implements marketing and sales-promotion plans, prepares units for promotional programmes, and encourages collection of information on customers and the competitive market
5. *Facilities and Safety Management* – supervises the overall condition of unit facilities to ensure operational acceptability and competitive readiness and establishes safety-management programmes.

In addition to ranking them in order of priority (as above), Umbreit also found from his research that in terms of major training needs, AMs themselves ranked HRM as their greatest barrier. This suggests that the behavioural dimension of indirectly leading at a distance was problematic to many newly promoted unit managers, who were more used to exercising daily control of operations.

Issues

- **Dependencies** – it could be argued that whilst Umbreit's model presents the five job aspects as mutually exclusive they are in fact inter-linked, with HRM being the major input driver to achieving the other job aspects
- **Skills** – Umbreit's model does not include the skills and competencies required for the role although his research does emphasise that AMs must learn essential skills such as networking for maximum resource access and delegation to effectively 'manage at a distance'
- **US Fast Food** – Umbreit's research (and that of many other US researchers after him) derives from the narrow band of US Fast Food.

How AMs can use this Model

Umbreit's seminal research provides a useful checklist of the fundamental job dimensions/aspects of the AM role (especially in food service). AMs can begin to calibrate their effectiveness against each dimension by asking themselves the following:

— Restaurant Operations – am I enforcing standards throughout multiple sites effectively through planning, checking, organising and delegating?
— HRM – am I spending enough time engaging, bonding, developing and coaching 'all the talents' within my team?
— Financial Management – am I concentrating upon the right KPIs and metrics within my businesses to move the P&L 'forwards'?
— Marketing and Promotions Management – are we implementing central marketing/promotions effectively? Do we understand our local markets/competition? Are we responding appropriately in a 'locally targeted' fashion?
— Facilities and Safety Management – are our units legally compliant and safe? Are we preserving the reputation of the company?

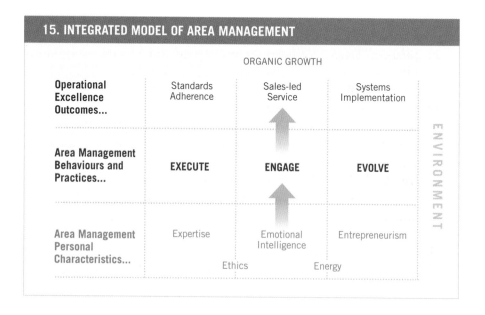

15. INTEGRATED MODEL OF AREA MANAGEMENT

Purpose

Edger's[10] Integrated Model of Area Management (IMAM) is a framework which, based on extensive empirical research, elucidates the key success factors of effective Area Managers who drive superior organic growth in both relative and absolute terms compared to their peers. It highlights the key linkages and dependencies between various activities and attributes, providing a guide for aspirant/ambitious AMs and their developers.

Components and Principles

The IMAM comprises four main cluster headings, with associated sub-components: environment (internal and external context), operational excellence outcomes, AM behaviours/practices and AM personal characteristics.

1. *Environment* – the first cluster seeks to place the AM in context (both internally and externally). For the role to be understood in any organisation, external factors such as economic conditions, regulatory framework, sector trends, level of competition (market share division), technological innovation and consumer behaviour trends must be factored into a dynamic understanding of the AM role. Internally, within the organisation, factors such as strategy, positioning, leadership, culture/politics, company history, structure/architecture, the marketing mix and HRM policies require consideration to understand the AM role within context.

2. *Operational Excellence Outcomes* – these are comprised of the three S's with vital subcomponents:
   a) *Sales-led Service Delivery* – unit-based HRM, service concept adherence, customer survey (or digital feedback) follow up, service promise delivery and complaints resolution etc.
   b) *Systems Implementation* (mainly BOH) – labour processes, standard operating procedures, product availability, stock and waste systems, sales and pricing monitoring, legal compliance/safety systems, ad hoc processes/change initiatives etc.
   c) *Standards Adherence* (mainly FOH) – merchandising and display, internal environmental management (cleanliness and 'set to go') and external environmental appearance etc.

3. *AM Behaviours/Practices* – includes the three E's:
   a) *Engage* (Team) – signature purpose driver ('famous for'), service ethos champion, talent builder, team facilitator and trust & recognition generator (has a strong dependency with sales-led service)
   b) *Execute* (Blueprint and Plan) – monitor & corrector, analytical linker and prioritiser, values standard bearer, strategic delegator, internal

---

10 Adapted from Edger, C. (2015) *Professional Area Management – Leading at a Distance in Multi-Unit Enterprises*, 2nd edition, Oxford: Libri; (2013) *International Multi-Unit Leadership – Developing Local Leaders in Multi-Site Operations,* Farnham: Gower; and (2012) *Effective Multi-Unit Leadership – Local Leadership in Multi-Site Situations,* Farnham: Gower.

networker and 'freedom within a frame' identifier (has a strong dependency with standards adherence)

c) *Evolve* (Operations and Offer) – mindset changer, benefits upseller, lead/champion appointer, continuous process improver and knowledge diffuser (has a strong dependency with systems implementation)

3. *AM Personal Characteristics* – includes technical, behavioural and cognitive attributes, otherwise known as the five E's:

a) *Emotional Intelligence* – self-awareness/control and mental toughness, follower insight/control, relationship and conflict management (strong dependency with Engage)

b) *Expertise* – domain knowledge (tacit and explicit) and cognitive numeracy (strong dependency with Execute)

c) *Entrepreneurship* – courage/curiosity and transmission/implementation (strong dependency with Evolve)

d) *Energy* – stamina (installed capacity to work) and passion/pace (underpins Engage, Execute and Evolve)

e) *Ethics* – values, morals and judgement (underpins Engage, Execute and Evolve).

Issues

- **Complexity** – at first sight this model can seem rather complex with multiple clusters, sub-components and linkages. Its benefit, however, is its attempt to connect attributes to practices and their associated outcomes.
- **Sectoral Application** – the IMAM has been constructed from research into AMs operating in retail, hospitality and leisure industries. Undoubtedly, some industries (such as hospitality) rank 'emotional' factors (sales-led service, engage and EI) above other sectors (such as 'hard' discounters within retail where a functional 'lean' philosophy predominates).

How AMs can use this Model

AMs can use this model in two ways:

- Benchmark – AMs can compare their activities, practices and attributes against this model to benchmark their professional practice
- Development – ambitious/aspirant AMs can use the IMAM as a development route map.

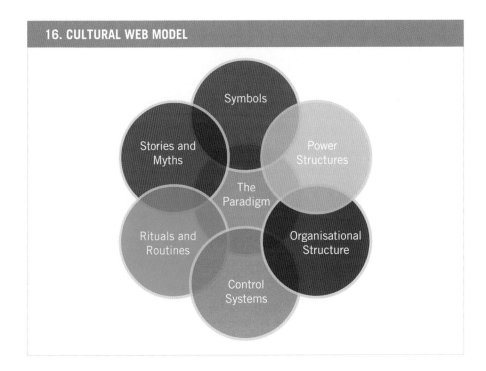

Purpose

Building upon Schein's[11] three levels of culture (artefacts, espoused values and basic underlying assumptions), Johnson and Scholes's[12] Cultural Web highlights the key internal cultural factors which influence the operations of an organisation.

Components and Principles

1. *The Paradigm* ('central belief system' or 'the way in which we do things around here') – the paradigm is derived from the six key factors determining a culture, comprising the main beliefs and assumptions held by members within an organisation. Cultural paradigms are idiosyncratic to organisations (manifesting for instance '*power*' or '*person*' cultures) although some scholars stress that isomorphic convergence persists amongst firms in some geographies due to the influence of dominant national cultural/business system influences.

2. *The Six Factors*
   a) *Rituals and Routines* – well-established formal and informal practices/ procedures and processes

---

11 Schein, E. (1985) *Organizational Culture and Leadership: A Dynamic Review*, San Francisco: Josey-Bass.
12 Adapted from Johnson, G., and Scholes, K. (1993) *Exploring Corporate Strategy*, London: Prentice Hall.

b) *Symbols* – artefacts of status such as job titles, offices and perks
c) *Stories* ('corporate memory') – apocryphal legends, tales and narratives regarding heroic successes or failure
d) *Organisational Structures* – key architectural characteristics (functional, centralised, hierarchical, matrix?)
e) *Control Systems* – bureaucratic output-led or values/ideological input-led?
f) *Power Structures* – professional elites (finance, marketing or operations?), patronage and recipients of reward.

Scholars conclude that the strongest cultures have aligned factors within the paradigm which give all employees a sense of confidence and well-being

Issues

- **Change** – meaningful change within organisations comes from changing the organisational DNA or 'shared belief' paradigm. The question is which factors (visible or invisible) should be tackled first? Some are harder to impact than others; for instance, erasing the corporate memory is far harder than changing structures.
- **External Influences** – this model is not only influenced by internal (leadership/history) effects but also by national culture/business systems forces. Hofstede's dimensions of national culture (power distance, uncertainty avoidance, individualism/collectivism, masculinity/femininity and long-/short-term orientation) all have profound effects on organisational cultures.
- **Micro-Cultures** – this model assumes a 'one culture' fits all dimension to organisations but inevitably (and certainly within international MUEs) due to distance, 'sub-branding' and semi-autonomous business units, sub-cultures within MUEs can flourish outside the dominant core.

How AMs can use the Model

- Organisational 'Sense-making' – AMs can use the model to 'make sense' of their organisational culture; often this is best done by making comparisons with other companies they are familiar with.
- District Sub-Culture – it is also useful for an AM to use as a checklist within his/her district to understand its idiosyncratic sub-culture – particularly in relation to artefacts (stories and symbols of success/failure). What AMs must try and do is erase 'narratives of failure' and supplant them with 'legends of success'! AMs can make a real difference to a district sub-culture, turning 'defeatist' cultures into vibrant, highly bonded 'can do' cultures. Create a culture of excellence by tangibly rewarding/recognising 'extra mile' behaviours (gifts, certificates, photos, time off etc.)

SECTION 2
ENGAGE
Team

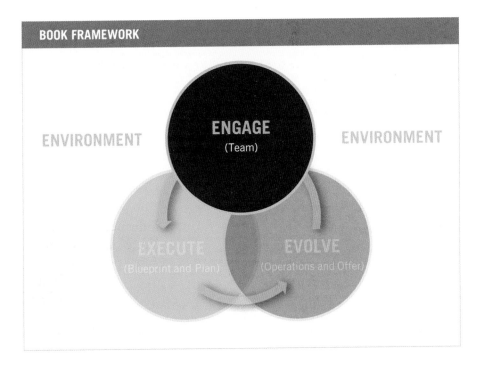

Having understood their environment, the *first* objective of Area Managers – given their focus upon delighting customers, achieving operational excellence and generating organic growth *without direct daily supervision* – is to **engage their team**. Winning hearts and minds – creating strong psychological bonding with their followers – is *the* fundamental precursor to creating a memorable service experiences, *executing* the brand blueprint/plan and *evolving* the offer/operations (see sections 3 and 4). The models in this section provide some guidance and insight into how AMs can effectively engage with their team.

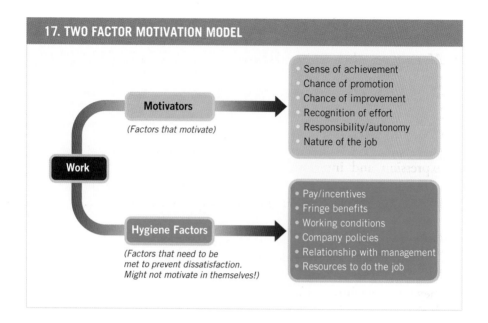

17. TWO FACTOR MOTIVATION MODEL

Motivators
(Factors that motivate)

- Sense of achievement
- Chance of promotion
- Chance of improvement
- Recognition of effort
- Responsibility/autonomy
- Nature of the job

Work

Hygiene Factors
(Factors that need to be met to prevent dissatisfaction. Might not motivate in themselves!)

- Pay/incentives
- Fringe benefits
- Working conditions
- Company policies
- Relationship with management
- Resources to do the job

Purpose

Herzberg's[13] seminal Two Factor Motivation Model (TFMM) addresses what drives human behaviour in the workplace, proposing a 'two factor' motivator-hygiene theory as an explanation for satisfaction/motivation. Its underlying assumption is that the two main drivers which shape satisfaction at work are completely different and, as such, require specific practice and policy responses from management.

Components and Principles

1. *Hygiene Factors* – these 'context' factors need to be in place first to prevent dissatisfaction. Although (for most people) they do not motivate behaviours, their improvement minimises the chances of 'base' dissatisfaction and can increase productivity/work outputs. Importantly, *motivators* (see below) will not work properly unless hygiene factors are properly accounted for, for individuals and/or teams. Hence organisations should ensure hygiene factors such as equitable reward, good working conditions, transparent/fair company policies, healthy boss–subordinate relations and sufficient resources to do the job (Maslow's[14] so-called physiological and security-based 'motivational

---

13 Adapted from 'Factors Affecting Job Attitudes as Reported in 12 Investigations' in Herzberg, F. (1987) 'One More Time: How Do You Motivate Employees?' *Harvard Business Review*, September–October.

14 Maslow, A.H. (1943) 'A theory of human motivation', *Psychological Review*, 50(4), pp.370–96.

needs') need to be in place so that workers are not extrinsically detached and demotivated.

2. *Motivators* – these 'content' factors are 'positive satisfiers' when they are present at work, leading to enhanced levels of discretionary effort by workers. They are only effective if they are underscored by appropriate hygiene factors. Elements in this motivational category include opportunities to feel a sense of achievement, meritocratic chances of promotion, due recognition for effort, the ability to display some self-expression and interesting dimensions to the job. These so-called intrinsic motivators also accord with Maslow's notions of 'higher level' human motivational requirement for 'self-actualisation'.

Issues

- **Enrichment or Enlargement?** – during the digital revolution, which has flattened structures further in MUEs, organisations have argued that they are 'enriching' workers' jobs through extra responsibilities and duties. This has inevitably led to high levels of dissatisfaction because this process – far from enriching roles – has merely enlarged jobs; a state that has served the organisation's rather than the individual's interests.
- **Individual Motivators** – the TFMM assumes that hygiene factors are not motivational in themselves; they are merely base context requirements that require satisfying in order for content motivators to work. However, for some individuals – due to personality type and circumstance – total reward is a prime motivator. For sure, different individuals have different needs, desires and attributes which mean that different subcomponents of the TFMM will have a more disproportionate effect than others.

How AMs can use this Model

AMs should pay particular attention to whether *hygiene* factors are in place before they apply/drive *motivator* factors; otherwise, they could be wasting precious time and effort. For instance, efforts to *satisfy* will be compromised by constant gripes/carping concerning poor working conditions and a lack of resources to do the job.

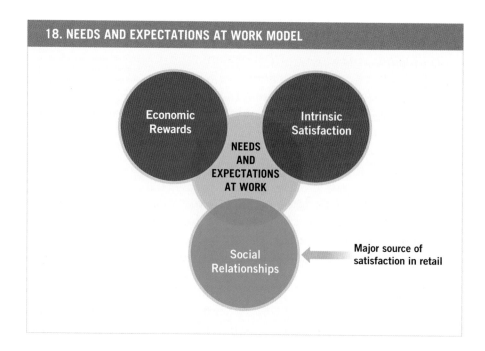

Purpose

The Needs and Expectations at Work Model[15] (NEWM) presents three simple components of the principal *satisfiers* at work according to an individual's needs and expectations.

Components and Principles

1. *Needs and Expectations at Work* – at the heart of the model, it is posited that an individual's satisfaction and performance are mediated by a pre-set number of needs and expectations. For instance, some workers have a basic need for extrinsic economic rewards (in hospitality, migrant and transitional workers, for instance) whilst others derive satisfaction principally through social relationships (older workers in retail, for instance). The main point of the model is that people have pre-set needs to work: if organisations and managers can meet worker expectations they stand a far greater chance of satisfying/motivating their charges.

5. *Satisfier Classifications*
   i. *Economic Rewards* – these satisfy an *individual's instrumental orientation* to work through factors such as the total reward package and job security guarantees

---

15 Adapted from Mullins, L.J. (2004) *Management and Organisational Behaviour*, Financial Times/Prentice Hall, p.473.

ii. Intrinsic Satisfaction – this meets a *personal orientation* to work where pleasure is gained from the nature of the work itself and the prospect of personal development/progression

iii. Social Relationships – this meets a *relational orientation* to work where satisfaction is enhanced from positive co-worker relations and strong teamship which meet specific worker needs for affiliation/belonging (particularly important in B2C social businesses where economic rewards are relatively low).

Issues

- **Compensatory Satisfiers** – the degree to which intrinsic satisfaction and social relationships can compensate for poor economic rewards is contingent upon the needs and expectations of workers. For some, these satisfiers will never overcome an expectation/need for generous total reward.
- **Balancing** – to the previous point, organisations need to review where the balance lies for their workers according to their relative needs and expectations (often framed by the personal requirements, transparency of the employment brand and its comparison with the competition).

How AMs can use this Model

For AMs operating in retail and hospitality, the concept of fostering strong relationships at the workplace level to compensate for a comparative lack of economic reward and long/unsocial hours must be taken seriously and acted upon. AMs should therefore ask themselves the following questions:

- Are my stores/units fun places to work?
- Do my teams get on well inside/outside work?
- Are we doing enough to engender a sense of *affiliation* through encouraging healthy social relationships (through events, charity drives, nights out, celebratory occasions etc.)?

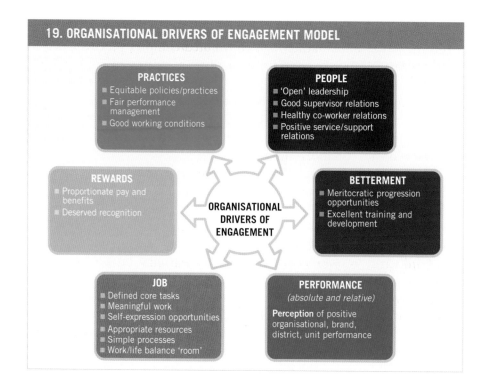

19. ORGANISATIONAL DRIVERS OF ENGAGEMENT MODEL

PRACTICES
- Equitable policies/practices
- Fair performance management
- Good working conditions

PEOPLE
- 'Open' leadership
- Good supervisor relations
- Healthy co-worker relations
- Positive service/support relations

REWARDS
- Proportionate pay and benefits
- Deserved recognition

ORGANISATIONAL DRIVERS OF ENGAGEMENT

BETTERMENT
- Meritocratic progression opportunities
- Excellent training and development

JOB
- Defined core tasks
- Meaningful work
- Self-expression opportunities
- Appropriate resources
- Simple processes
- Work/life balance 'room'

PERFORMANCE
(absolute and relative)

Perception of positive organisational, brand, district, unit performance

Purpose

Organisational engagement denotes a positive relationship or 'psychological attachment' between an employee and his/her organisation. Highly engaged employees are likely to be committed to their work and the organisation's goals – displaying high levels of discretionary effort – thus contributing to progressing/enhancing the organisation's levels of performance/reputation. Employees with low levels of engagement have the reverse effect – they degrade/undermine the organisation's interests. The Organisational Drivers of Engagement Model (ODEM) is an aggregation of 22 of the key academic and consultant models that seek to illustrate the key forces that build/sustain organisational engagement.

Components and Principles

The ODEM comprises a number of extrinsic ('hygiene') factors and intrinsic ('self-actualising') factors:

1. **Job** – employee engagement is enhanced when the job undertaken has defined core tasks so that employees can perform to pre-set requirements and standards (without fear of consequences), the work itself is meaningful (having benefits for both the employee and organisation), opportunities are afforded for autonomy/self-expression (so-called

'freedom within a frame'), appropriate resources are provided ('tools to do the job'), simple rather than convoluted/complex processes prevail (that don't require constant 'fixing') and room exists within the role for a healthy work–life balance.

2. *Rewards* – a major hygiene factor, engagement, can be bolstered if the total pay and benefits package is perceived to be proportionate and fair by employees; regular/frequent recognition which supplements equitable reward further enhances engagement.

3. *Practices* – engagement is augmented by transparent/honest/fair policies and practices, accompanied by even-handed performance management systems and acceptable working conditions.

4. *People* – leadership which fosters a trusting environment through clear/open communications in addition to excellent superior–subordinate, co-worker and support relations further enhances engagement.

5. *Betterment* – progression is not a key objective for some employees (due to capability/aspiration), but the existence of meritocratic avenues for betterment, accompanied by accredited training and development programmes, acts as a formidable engagement device.

6. *Performance* – a significant factor in engagement (although neglected by many models) is the successful absolute/relative performance of the organisation, strategic business unit, team or individual. Perceptions of performance success (either through sales or profit growth) are an important mediator in the engagement equation.

Issues

- **Engagement–Profit Linkage** – there is no empirical proof that high levels of engagement lead to positive financial outcomes. Happy people (who might be ignorant about the company's performance) do not necessarily drive superior performance if, say, the firm's business model is broken. Rather, evidence regarding reverse causality is more compelling – successful and profitable concerns create happy people! Hence the importance of the inclusion of factor #6, 'performance', in the ODEM above.

- **Deadly Combinations** – often firms will get many of the macro-drivers right but engagement might be derailed at a local level by factors such as toxic manager–worker relations. Several studies have highlighted the importance of boss–subordinate relations as the main mediator of satisfaction (i.e. people leave bosses rather than organisations!) – companies must ensure that managers are fully trained/equipped to lead/manage effectively.

How AMs can use this Model

AMs can use this model in tandem with their employee survey results (if these exist) to understand where and for what reasons engagement is either working or breaking down.

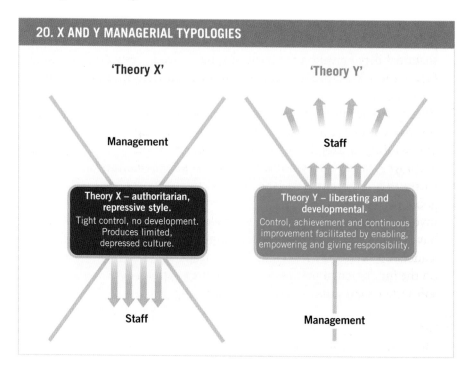

Purpose

McGregor's[16] Managerial X and Y Theory has been the basis for much of the leadership literature that has flowed from scholarly enquiry since the 1960s, as well as the underpinning of much of the HRM and organisational behaviour fields. In short, the model addresses *managerial perceptions* of employees which, in turn, influence *managerial styles* and the way in which managers go about *motivating employees*.

Components and Principles

1. *Theory X* – managers who fall within this typology fundamentally believe that most employees will slack off given half a chance and inherently seek ways in which to avoid working productively! Theory X managers therefore believe that the best form of motivation lies in

16 Adapted from McGregor, D., 'The Human Side of Enterprise', reproduced in D.S. Pugh (ed.) (1990) *Organization Theory*, Penguin.

deploying/exercising tight spans of control and high levels of compliance, and imposing stretching incentive targets. This managerial approach (described as Transactional or Path–Goal Leadership by other academics) has been found – if excessively applied – to lead to high levels of mistrust, resistance and demotivation; although in certain circumstances (such as turnaround events or extreme crises) a Theory X approach can result in positive outcomes. Question marks remain, however, regarding its sustainability given the basic human need (especially amongst Generation Y employees) for autonomy, self-determination and self-expression.

2. *Theory Y* – according to this theoretical perspective, Theory Y managers positively believe their charges to be intrinsically aspirational, motivated and willing to exercise self-control. Theory Y managers believe that employees seek – in Maslowian terms – self-actualisation from their work; they inherently wish to succeed in the workplace, seek to do a good job, responding positively to open communications, high levels of involvement and quality training/development programmes. Academics have expanded this notion into concepts such as transformational leadership, strategic HRM and servant leadership, all of which are based on the fundamental premise that employees respond better to trust-based soft rather than punitive hard leadership approaches.

Issues

- **Organisational Situation** – the firm's performance (whether positive or parlous) will inevitably have a major contingent effect on managerial styles at any particular time.
- **Supervisor/Subordinate Relations** – according to leader–member exchange (LMX) theory, relations between managers and employees are unique and specific, varying on an individual basis. Different employees will respond differently to a carrot or stick approach depending on attitude, profile, personality, ambition, age, situation etc.

How AMs can use this Model

AMs should use this model to ask themselves the following questions:

- Does your perception of employee behaviour fall within the Theory X ('inherently lazy') or Theory Y ('inherently committed to doing a good job') categorisation? How does this affect your managerial style?
- What are the consequences of your negative or positive perceptions of employee motivation?

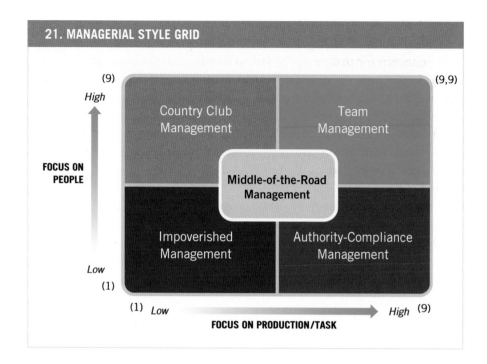

Purpose

The Managerial Style Grid[17] (MSG) enables managers to plot their leadership style in accordance with the degree to which they focus on the human 'input' dimension (people) juxtaposed against a concern for hard task 'outputs' (production). Its underlying premise is that managers have a natural style of managing (see the X and Y Managerial Typology Model, above); understanding where it lies increases self-awareness of its efficacy/effectiveness.

Components and Principles

1. *Grid Dimensions*

   a) *Focus on People* – the extent to which a manager displays a 'leader's concern' for his/her subordinates' desires, aspirations, needs and other attributes in order to motivate his/her charges to perform.

   b) *Focus on Production/Task* – the extent to which a manager focuses upon compliance, control, structure, organisation and resource allocation to achieve targets.

---

17 Adapted from Blake, R., Mouton, J., Barnes, L., and Greiner, L. (1964) 'Breakthrough in Organisation Development', *Harvard Business Review*, November–December, p.136.

2. *Style Typologies*

a) *Impoverished Management* (1,1) – managers with this style have little concern for people or the task at hand!

b) *Authority/Compliance Management* (9,1) – managers in this grid adopt a purely transactional production/task approach in order to achieve results.

c) *Middle-of-the-Road Management* (5,5) – managers have an average predisposition to achieving results through 'mildly' focussing upon people and production.

d) *Country Club Management* (1,9) – managers rely totally upon high context relationships to get results, having little interest in the task detail.

e) *Team Management* (9,9) – managers have a simultaneously high interest in 'leading' people and 'managing' the task for optimal performance outcomes.

Issues

- **Situational 'Fit'** – in contrast to fixed style of leadership models, contingent models argue that adopting any particular style is not wrong in itself as long as it fits with the situation. The MSG hints at compliance, country-club and middle-of-the-road management as being sub-optimal however 'the time' or the situation might require managers to adopt certain styles of leadership; at certain junctures, therefore, these styles might be appropriate. Thus, in times of crisis or situations requiring a quick turnaround, a requirement for authority/compliance-based managerial approaches might be essential. The question – of course – is whether or not managers have the ability to adapt their style to any given situation!

- **Perception** – managers often lack the self-awareness to understand where their dominant 'default' style lies. A misperception, commonly held by many managers, is that their dominant style is team management (9,9), when in reality they lie at other extremes of the grid. Managers must utilise and absorb analysis from tools such as EOS (Employee Opinion Surveys) and 360-degree feedback to understand where their subordinates really believe they sit.

- **Context** – managerial styles are not only the by-product of manager personality, learning and capability; they are also heavily influenced by dominant cultural paradigms within their respective organisations ('hard' production orientation or 'soft' people orientation).

How AMs can use this Model

This model can be used by AMs to raise their own awareness of their style, when considering whether it is fit for purpose given the *situation* of their district or certain individuals. It can then provide a basis for development coaching and EI training if concern for people is low, for instance.

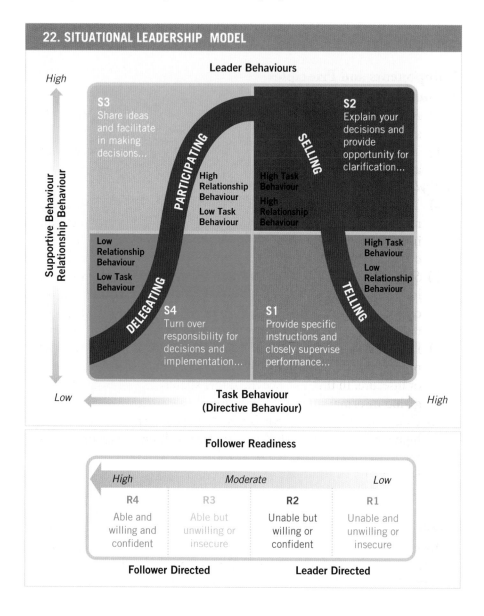

Purpose

The Situational Leadership Model (SLM)[18] is a contingency-based ('fit' or match) model of leadership which is premised upon *leadership styles* being effective (either through strong direction or delegation) according to levels of follower readiness (ranging from unable/unwilling to able/willing). This model is important because of its implicit thesis that there is no ideal type of leadership; rather, the best leadership approach (either task-led or relationship-led) depends on the situation.

Components and Principles

1. *Guiding Dimensions*

a) *Relationship Behaviour* – the degree to which the leader deploys 'soft' social/supportive behaviour.

b) *Task Behaviour* – the degree to which a leader explicitly commands and directs subordinates.

2. *Styles (S) and Readiness 'Fit'*

a) *Telling (S1)* – this style is used subordinates with low levels of readiness (R1) – those that are unable, unwilling or insecure. It involves issuing clear instructions and the close monitoring of task completion.

b) *Selling (S2)* – this style is deployed for subordinates with moderate levels of readiness (R2) – those that are unable but willing or confident. Here leaders should provide some instruction regarding task completion but allow opportunities for involvement/discussion.

c) Participating (S3) – this style is used for followers who have a moderate level of readiness (R3) – those that are able but unwilling or insecure. In this instance the leader should act as a facilitator/coach giving informal support to increase engagement/confidence.

d) Delegating (S4) – this style is best deployed for followers who have a high level of readiness (R4) and are able, willing and confident. Here the leader should delegate responsibility (but not accountability) for important tasks/initiatives to maintain levels of engagement/ motivation.

Issues

- **Readiness Flux** – leaders need to be cognisant of the fact that followers can transition both ways on the readiness scale according to attitude and capability. An R4 follower today can – due to immense change or altered personal circumstances – transition rapidly to an R1 state. To this extent

---

18 Adapted from Hersey, P. (1984) *The Situational Leader*, Escondido, CA: Center for Leadership Studies, p.63.

subordinate readiness cannot be seen as a static but a dynamic construct and leaders should be capable of 'spotting the signs' and adapting their leadership style accordingly.

- **Measurement** – how do leaders calibrate levels of follower readiness? Skills can be dispassionately assessed but attitude is a far more fickle dimension to calibrate. Leaders must therefore become attuned to watching behavioural signals to read where followers really are on the attitudinal spectrum.
- **Flexibility** – this model makes a major presupposition that leaders can adapt their style to meld with specific 'leadership situations'. The truth is that many managers have a one-size-fits-all leadership approach; therefore, many managers will require coaching/observation to 'bring on' their 'leadership style matching' skills (something that many organisations fail to provide!).

How AMs can use this Model

AMs should plot where they think their subordinates are with regards to levels of readiness on the SLM and ask themselves, 'Am I deploying the right match of leadership style (S1–S4) to get the best out of each individual follower given their respective readiness (R1–R4) positioning?'

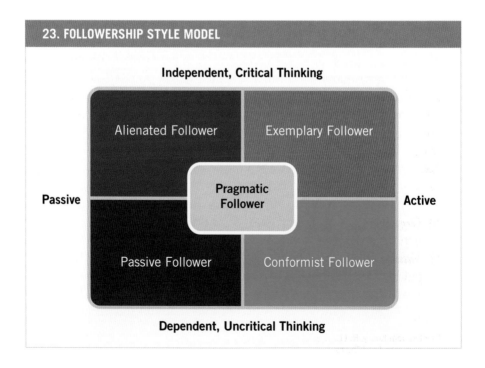

23. FOLLOWERSHIP STYLE MODEL

Independent, Critical Thinking

Alienated Follower

Exemplary Follower

Pragmatic Follower

Passive

Active

Passive Follower

Conformist Follower

Dependent, Uncritical Thinking

Purpose

Kelley's[19] Followership Style Model (FSM) highlights five dominant follower engagement styles (alienated, exemplary, passive, conformist and pragmatic) which are attributable to a need to be dependent or independent, critical or uncritically thinking, or active or passive in disposition. The FSM is useful for any follower (and most employees are followers!) who wishes to review their type of follower engagement style with their superior in order to reflect on its impact and potential outcomes.

Components and Principles

In order to help employees understand what type of follower style they have, Kelley poses a number of rhetorical questions:

1. *Alienated Follower* – are you troublesome, cynical or negative? Do you have a chip on your shoulder – are you a 'rebel without a cause'? Are you headstrong and lacking in judgement? Do you fail in being a team player? Are you adversarial to the point of being hostile?

2. *Conformist Follower* – do you lack your own ideas? Are you obsequious and ingratiating? Are you unwilling to take an unpopular decision and stick to it? Are you averse to conflict, even at the risk of going over the cliff with the group?

3. *Passive Follower* – are you putting in 'your time' but little else? Don't you do your share? Do you require an inordinate amount of supervision relative to your contribution? Do you follow the crowd without wondering why?

4. *Pragmatic Follower* – are you good at playing political games and bargaining to maximise your own self-interest? Are you averse to risk and prone to covering your tracks? Are you good at carrying out assignments with middling enthusiasm and in a mediocre fashion? Are you a bureaucrat who adheres to the letter of the law rather than the spirit?

5. *Exemplary Follower* – key attributes:
   a) *Job Skills* – focus and commitment, competence in critical path activities and initiative in increasing their value to the organisation
   b) *Organisation Skills* – team members, forger of organisational networks; leaders!
   c) *Values Component* – Possessors of a 'courageous conscience' which guides activities and relationships.

---

19 Adapted from Kelley, R. (1992) *The Power of Followership: How to Create Leaders People Want to Follow and Followers Who Lead Themselves*, Bantam Doubleday (Dell Publishing Group).

Issues

- **Behavioural Transition** – the FSM can be interpreted as a static manifestation of style when, in actual fact, followers can adjust their styles according to situation.
- **Inaccurate Self-perception** – managers are notoriously bad at judging how they are actually perceived due to their own false misconception and the lack of honest appraisal from peers/superiors. Some managers will categorise themselves erroneously (e.g., as exemplary rather than alienated!) and will – in time – suffer dire consequences as a result.

How AMs can use this Model

AMs should reflect upon the fact that their regional/brand directors will value tolerance, maturity, flexibility, critical thinking and energy from their followers – attributes which fall directly into the exemplary follower category! Thus, AMs should critically evaluate where they really lie in terms of follower style and engagement and – if they fall outside the exemplary follower category – question a) how sustainable their current follower mindset is (given the potential consequences) and b) how they can augment/transition their mindset into an exemplary follower frame?

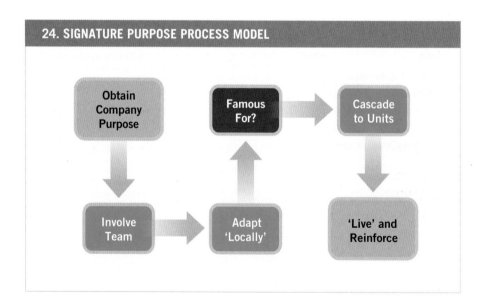

24. SIGNATURE PURPOSE PROCESS MODEL

- Obtain Company Purpose
- Famous For?
- Cascade to Units
- Involve Team
- Adapt 'Locally'
- 'Live' and Reinforce

Purpose

Managers – particularly in dispersed multi-site entities – should aim to foster a sense of meaning and purpose for their teams, which performs the role of engendering clarity, motivation and (ideally) self-regulating behaviour. In addition, it can also, first, serve as a bridge between the corporate entity and local operations and, second, create a 'why' – which is particularly important for Generation Y employees, who seek real meaning from their work! The Signature Purpose Model suggests a means by which local management can go about crafting and disseminating a compelling local vision.

Components and Principles

The Signature Purpose Model (SPM) is fundamentally a process framework which illustrates how AMs might tackle creating a bonding, resonant signature purpose with their team. The key to its success, however, is that it should have a signature (proprietorial) feel – being created, owned and bought into by all team members. In addition, it should be aspirational in the sense that it should be a statement of what the district will be 'famous for' (indeed, it should be a statement that encapsulates what the AM and his/her team want to be known and admired for within the organisation AND by their customers). The model's process steps are as follows:

1. *Obtain Company Purpose* – establish what it is (e.g. Domino's Pizza: 'Sell More Pizza, Have More Fun')
2. *Involve Team* – gather team together at an appropriate forum that will allow appropriate time and space for consideration of the district's signature purpose
3. *Adapt Locally* – look at the corporate purpose: can it be iterated for local resonance?
4. *Famous For…* – make sure that the agreed purpose for the district is really a statement about what you wish to be known and admired for; brevity and emotional language will make it more memorable! Address the question, 'would my team get out of bed in the morning to try and achieve this?'
5. *Cascade to Units* – ensure the signature purpose is cascaded to team member level
6. *'Live' and Reinforce* – use it in your communications, everyday language and be the standard bearer for what you want your district to be famous for!

Issues

- **Realism** – stating that you 'want to be known as the No1 hospitality/retail operators in the UK' is vacuous and vague. Make sure your signature purpose – whilst aspirational and memorable – is achievable.
- **Tactics** – a signature purpose must be backed up by a plan and tactics which will enable it to be realised and sustained. Often grand statements

of intent are just that – unrealisable because insufficient attention has been given to the inputs required to get organisations where they want to be!

How AMs can use this Model

The whole point of crafting/adopting a signature purpose is to bond/motivate the team and ensure that the district is FAMOUS for something, pulling together to achieve something of REAL MEANING. AMs should – when assuming the reins of a new district or looking to 'refresh' their existing district – utilise the process in the model above. Don't worry if it isn't quite right first time around – park the issue and try again with the team some other time. More haste, less speed will produce a more enduring/impactful result.

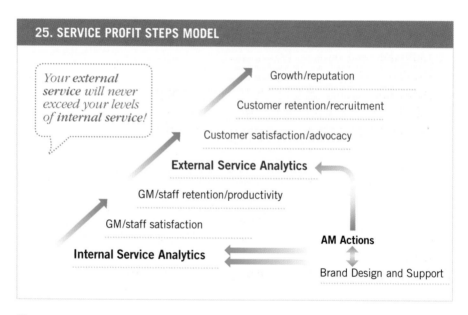

Purpose

The Service Profit Steps Model (SPS) illustrates the strong links between internal and external service quality and firm performance. Service is one of the major controllables for AMs and the extent to which user experiences are memorable (particularly in restaurant hospitality where intangible memories rather than a tangible products are 'carried out of the door' by customers) is a major determinant of success. The AM's role in troubleshooting, chasing and improving levels of *internal* service into his/her units from a range of support providers is absolutely fundamental to *externally* perceived service quality. Remember, your levels of external service will rarely exceed your levels of internal service!

Components and Principles

The multiple phases in the SPS start with the degree of support and 'set-up' provided by the organisation – mediated/monitored by the AM:

1. ***Brand Design and Support*** – includes product design (service delivery system and brand/operational strategy), workplace design, HRM systems and appropriate resources/processes (machinery, technology and 'tools') to serve customers.

2. ***Internal Service Analytics*** – ideally AMs should measure/monitor internal service quality (levels of organisational support) directly through % provision of required resources ('people and kit'), speed of defect resolutions (i.e. maintenance), % information accuracy, support service response times (especially during peak sessions and over weekends!), number of unwarranted time wasting 'requests' and feedback from GM/staff satisfaction surveys.

3. ***AM Actions*** – having garnered internal service information from both qualitative and quantitative sources, AMs will act as a troubleshooter/'fixer', resolving internal service issues to 'ease the burden' for their teams.

4. ***GM/Staff Satisfaction*** – the speedy resolution of internal service delivery 'bumps' will increase satisfaction levels at a unit level, increase the AM's 'follower capital' and release teams to concentrate on the customer.

5. ***GM/Staff Retention/Productivity*** – satisfaction will increase the 'propensity to stay' and productivity/discretionary effort/quality work.

6. ***External Service Analytics*** – these should be positive (high NPS, low complaints, positive 'word of mouse' etc.). Again, AMs should scrutinise these metrics to consider remedial actions that will improve certain scores.

7. ***Customer Satisfaction/Advocacy*** – a great product delivered by motivated, well-organised teams should lead to raving advocates of the brand/unit.

8. ***Customer Retention/Recruitment*** – these raving fans will become loyal customers, also co-opting non-users and lapsed users through word of mouth/mouse.

9. ***Growth/Reputation*** – if the preceding steps have been followed then, hypothetically, the brand's reputation and financials are enhanced.

Issues

- **Performance Linkages** – service takes place within a specific brand/product context. Excellent service will not trump a poor, overpriced product. Therefore, service has a relative rather than absolute connection with performance.

- **Data** – getting hold of internal service analytics is problematic (companies normally focus upon external analytics). The AM must therefore be prepared to scrutinise qualitative data to locate/fix breakdown patterns: stories, complaints, 'cries for help'!

How AMs can use this Model
- Internal Service Analytics – analyse your internal service 'quality detractors' – what are the greatest obstacles/problems for your teams?
- Action – resolve internal service issues by troubleshooting, using your internal networks and delegating key tasks to be chased up.
- External Service Analytics – keep analysing customer feedback and behaviour and resolve the controllable elements of poor metrics (internal service breakdowns, GM/team dissatisfaction, levels of capability/ motivation etc.).

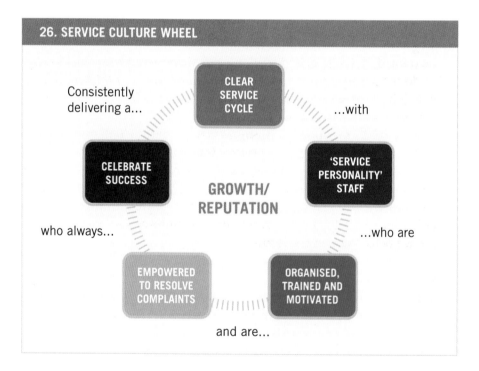

Purpose
The Service Culture Wheel Model (SCWM) is a representation of the key elements that lead to a positive service culture at unit level within MUEs. Its sequential stages represent the various interdependent attributes of unit-level service cultures that will result in satisfying/memorable service experiences for guests/users; ultimately resulting in retention, loyalty,

advocacy and new-user recruitment, resulting (hypothetically) in higher sales and a better reputation.

Key Components and Principles

The SCWM highlights five interlinked stages involved in constructing a successful unit-level service culture:

1. *Clear Service Cycle* – the chain of service (customer 'touches' from welcome to exit) should be simple and easily understood by service providers involved at key moments of the customer order fulfilment process.

2. *Service Personality Staff* – staff should be recruited into service-based businesses on the basis of 'will' – not purely 'skill'. Staff who gain pleasure from serving others and working as a team can be trained to despatch the technical aspects of the role within service organisations. Recruiting for 'emotional contagion' is more important than hiring for pure technical ability.

3. *Organised, Trained and Motivated* – following immersion staff should be trained, developed, deployed, rewarded and resourced with the tools to do the job to expedite their duties with passion and efficiency. Their core job purpose should be made clear and unambiguous (e.g. waitress: 'to make customers happy!').

4. *Empowered to Resolve Complaints* – immediate, on-the-spot rectification of problems or service breakdowns will not only (in most cases) exceed customer expectations, it will result in positive perceptions about the brand/product.

5. *Celebrate Success* – post-session recognition of great service 'moments' either individually or on a team basis will reinforce and bolster positive service behaviours in the future.

Issues

- **Deadly Combinations** – if the product, price or environment is poor, service will only go part way to recovering customer perceptions. Product, price, environment and service are part of a balanced equation that (depending on the positioning of the brand) has an overall mediating effect on overall customer perceptions (see Value Proposition Model).

- **Employment Brand** – in theory, AMs/GMs should always hire the best 'service personality' staff from the external labour market. The reality (given the poor perception of retail, with its low level of pay and unsocial hours) organisations will be simultaneously competing for talent with many losing out due to defective employment branding (caused through 'lean HRM').

How AMs can use this Model

AMs should ask themselves the following questions:
- Is the chain of service clear and documented in simple terms for frontline service providers?
- Are my GMs and their management teams hiring 'service personalities'?
- Are we organising/motivating/training our service providers appropriately?
- Are our service providers aware of our rectification protocol – are they properly empowered/equipped to resolve issues 'on the spot'?
- Do we celebrate WOW! service moments with the team? Are we recognising team members with rewards that they can show or boast about to their friends and families (thereby increasing their levels of pride self-esteem)?

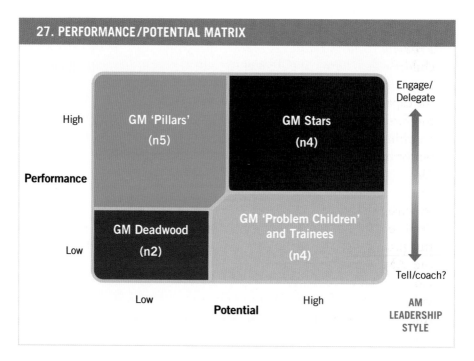

Purpose

The Performance/Potential Matrix Model (PPM) is a useful tool for AMs to make a quick assessment of their key reports and their relative capabilities. It helps them to decide where to concentrate their effort in pursuance of increasing the performance of their district, highlighting how their leadership/managerial style will vary according to various GM (General Manager) typologies; tell/coach (deadwood and trainees) and engage/delegate (pillars/stars).

Components and Principles

Given the critical importance of the GM within the MUE (due to its dispersed organisational form and high reliance on consistency of execution), the AM needs to ensure that (s)he has a good balance of GM talent led/managed in the most appropriate manner:

1. *Stars* – this cohort has high performance and potential levels. AMs must engage with this cohort immediately after taking over a district in order to co-opt them in terms of delegation/support; in some instances appointing them as leads, champions or cluster heads.

2. *Pillars* – these GMs exhibit high levels of performance but lower potential (either through aspiration or capability). Nonetheless, as key members of the team (who are more likely to stay in situ than the stars), AMs must actively engage with this group and – crucially – continue to develop and nurture this population for motivational purposes. Utilising this cohort as process leads/champions is a major way of harnessing their talents.

3. *Problem Children and Trainees* – this group is made up of 'problem children' who have the potential to transition into the stars category or regress (due to attitude) into the deadwood box, and trainees who have the capability to be moulded into the high-performing district leaders of the future. Both categories require an element of telling and intensive coaching so that their potential can be converted into high levels of performance.

4. *Deadwood* – generally due to attitudinal disposition (which has turned them into toxics, resistors or saboteurs) or a severe lack of capability (due to changes to the service concept or technological innovation), deadwood GMs must be addressed and cleared out by AMs. However, this process of deforestation (which might already be underway when the AM takes over the district) needs to be handled with care. Courageous conversations, intensive performance management and extensive advice from HR professionals are required for optimal results (their exit at no cost to the business).

Issues

- **Judgement** – often AM perceptions will vary concerning which category GMs fall into. One AM's star is another AM's pillar! All judgements must be based around empirical observation of outputs, actions and behaviours.
- **AM Style** – this model makes the assumption that AMs can adapt their style and approach to any given cohort. The truth is that many AMs are incapable of changing their style, constantly defaulting to inflexible, one-dimensional approaches to management.

How AMs can use this Model

AMs should ask themselves:

- Stars – am I giving them enough challenge, exposure and responsibility to progress to the next career stage?
- Pillars – am I sufficiently recognising their invaluable contribution by utilising/drawing upon their expertise/talents?
- Problem Children and Trainees – am I spending enough time coaching, moulding and shaping this cohort to ensure that they become stars of the future?
- Deadwood – is the process of deforestation being conducted swiftly, professionally and legally?

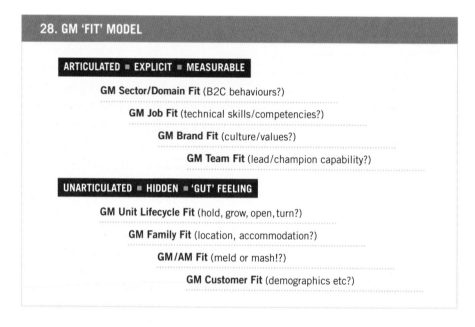

Purpose

Properly matching GMs to the right sites within a district is one of the most important jobs of the AM. The right GM, in the right site at the right time, can result in a 10% sales dividend in functionally led retail and a 30% uplift in emotionally based hospitality if the previous incumbents were underperforming against the site's true potential. This GM 'Fit' Model (GMFM) is sub-divided into two areas: articulated/explicit and unarticulated/hidden measures of fit that the AM must consider when making appointments/assessments.

Components and Principles

The GMFM provides a checklist and a range of questions that the AM should utilise/consider during GM appointment processes:

1. *Articulated/Explicit/Measurable Factors* (things that are generally recorded)

   a) *Sectoral/Domain Fit* – is this GM temperamentally suited to a B2C environment? Does this candidate have a 'happy' service-orientated personality – i.e. does (s)he derive pleasure from serving/'doing things' for others?

   b) *Brand Fit* – does this GM have a value set that chimes with those of the organisation/brand? Will this GM fit the culture of the organisation/brand?

   c) *Job Fit*

      ○ Behavioural Skills
      - *Intrinsic motivation* – does this GM have appropriate *needs and expectations* that will be fulfilled by the job role itself? Is s(he) realistic about the constraints surrounding the job but intrinsically motivated by the challenges and opportunities of leading a team of service providers?
      - *Team Leadership/Management* – does (s)he have the capability to select, motivate and lead a team/sections of service providers, especially in units with a small management structure? Is (s)he capable of prioritising, planning, organising and delegating tasks?
      - *Customer Service* – does s(he) have positive/happy social and interpersonal skills backed up with a real passion for satisfying customer needs? Is this person capable of going the extra mile, generating *memorable experiences* for customers (especially in hospitality where intangible memories – rather than tangible goods – are often all the customer leaves with).

      ○ Technical Skills
      - *Technical/Craft* – does (s)he have craft (such as food production in casual dining), merchanting (layout and display) and/or technical (volume and capacity management) skills that will enable greater efficiency and effectiveness?
      - *Administrative/Blueprint* – does (s)he have adequate administrative skills in order to apply/monitor blueprinted systems and processes?

- Cognitive Skills
    - *Thinking* – does (s)he have the ability to interpret and critically analyse quantitative and qualitative data in order to take remedial action?
    - *Numeracy* – given the fact that performance is measured through financial metrics and tracked through key data reports, is (s)he financially literate? Moreover can (s)he read the dependencies between the P&L and other input metrics?

d) *Team Fit* – in addition to attitude and aptitude at an individual level, contributing to the wider team is important, with AMs asking themselves two questions: will this appointment improve the balance of skills, personalities and capabilities within my team? Will this appointment infuse the team with more energy and drive?

2. ***Unarticulated/Hidden/Gut Feeling Factors*** (things AMs have to 'drill down' to establish)
    a) *Store Lifecycle Fit*
        - *Growth (Investment)* – does the GM have the required level of energy and passion to leverage the store through a high growth drive?
        - *Maturity* – is the GM suited to sustaining the store through a period of under-investment and 'milking'?
        - *Turnaround* – does the GM have the resilience, experience and/or drive to transform an underperforming site?
        - *Start-Up* – does the GM have the capability to deal with the uncertainty, ambiguity, fluidity of a start-up situation?

    b) *Family Fit* – does this site fit with the requirements/expectations of the GM's partner/family?
    c) *AM Fit* – can I work with this person? Will we mesh or mash? Will (s)he irritate me!? Do we have any personal chemistry? Is this GM capable of value-added followership i.e. is (s)he reliable, tolerant (of my behaviour!), flexible, a critical thinker, open to learning and development etc.?
    d) *Customer Fit* – does this GM fit with the customer profile in this particular location?

Issues

- **Art and Science** – the process of hiring the right GM for the right site is an art and a science. It is likely that AMs that have been in the role for longer will have better tacit knowledge on optimal fit based on experiences of prior successes/failures.

- **Priority** – this model outlines a number of factors that are important in establishing GM 'fit', but which ones are the most important? Clearly B2C fit is taken as a given but the context of the brand, site (its scale, position and possible segmentation) and the wider district team must be well understood, for prioritisation of key factors to occur.
- **Expediency** – often, because of the dynamic pace of retail, vacancies will occur and the AM will have to take sub-optimal fit decisions on the hoof just to keep the unit open and trading! The GMFM assumes that the AM has the time and space to consider all these variables when there is a need to quickly appoint 'somebody with a pulse'! In these circumstances, AMs would be well advised to appoint Relief GMs or temporary acting GMs before they find the best possible match. Bad appointments are highly costly: easy to make and hard to unpick (appoint in haste, repent at leisure!).

How AMs can use this Model

The GMFM helps AMs to consider some of the main contingent variables relating to successful GM appointments. It is useful because, often, generic competency frameworks prescribed by HR are unfit for purpose because they fail to capture unarticulated/hidden requirements for best fit. AMs should use this model as a prompt/guide to consider appointments or succession planning requirements (see next model).

---

29. SUCCESSION PLANNING FRAMEWORK

ROLE: **KITCHEN MANAGER**
Current holder: John Smith

Successors	Travel/Relocate?	Ready Date?	Major Development Needs?	PDP?
1 **R. Kennedy**	In-situ	0-3 months	Planning	Yes
2 **S. Jones (RL)**	Yes (15 miles)	6-9 months	Finance	Yes
3 **C. Manka (GH)**	Yes (23 miles)	9-12 months	Written English	Yes

External Recruitment?
Target Date –

Purpose

The Succession Planning Framework (SPF) is a simple tool that sits behind key talent requirements of the district, providing AMs with essential data on 'benchstrength': where contingency cover exists and potential gaps remain requiring urgent attention.

Components and Principles

1. ***Role*** –a key role on the district
2. ***Current Holder*** – name (and estimated duration until exit?)
3. ***Successors***
   a) Names – likely replacement
   b) Travel/Relocate? – confirm mobility
   c) Readiness – likely timescale
   d) Development Needs – particularly for this role
   e) PDP – is training and development built into a Personal Development Plan?

4. ***External Recruitment*** – is a headhunting exercise in the local area required by the AM (cold-calling competitor units) or an agency?

Issues

* **Hoarding** – in spite of an organisation's best efforts, an AM's peers will hoard their best people, so growing your own talent is an essential AM exercise.
* **Forced Changes** – AMs need to proactively manage key people changes and site 'role-swaps' in order to ramp up performance; waiting for 'voluntary turnover' is not an option in some business situations! It is unlikely that AMs will take a transparent talent bank/succession planning approach to what will be an extremely delicate process of 'district chess'.

How AMs can use this Tool

If nothing else, this simple tool makes AMs look at their human capital in relation to the performance of the district and helps him/her line up alternatives in the event of surprise, planned or forced departures. As vacancies occur (through chance or force), the AM needs to have a range of viable options which will drive performance and growth.

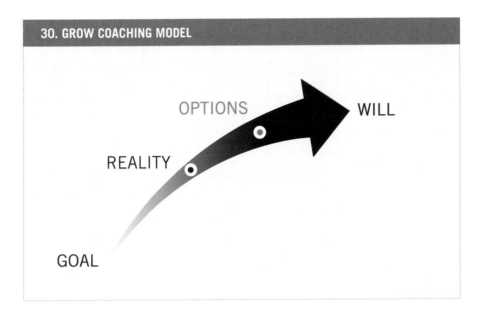

Purpose

The GROW Model[20] is a sequential coaching method which leader–coaches can use with their subordinates in order to get them to solve their *own* issues (fostering BOTH AWARENESS AND ACCOUNTABILITY). The GROW technique is intended to increase subordinate ownership/accountability and (in the case of AMs) saves managers having to perpetually 'hand hold' and become debilitated by constantly solving the problems of others.

Components and Principles

Great leader–coaches help their subordinates to define what they want or need to improve (through *goal* definition), to understand what is currently happening or getting in the way (the *reality* of situation), to explore a range of strategies that might resolve issues or blockages (resolution *options*) and to commit to a plan of action (*will to get it done*). Open questions that the leader–coach can use to facilitate the discussion include:

1. **GOAL** – what do you want to achieve? When do you want to achieve it by? What are you looking for from me?
2. **REALITY** – what is happening now? On a scale of one to ten, where are you now? What have you done about it? What are the major constraints

---

20 Adapted from Downey, M. (2003) *Effective Coaching: Lessons from the Coach's Coach*, Texere Publishing, and Whitmore, J. (2009) *Coaching for Performance: GROWing Human Potential and Purpose – The Principles and Practices of Coaching and Leadership*, 4th edition, London: Nicholas Brealey.

to finding a way forwards? What is the evidence for that? What would you advise a friend to do if they were in your shoes?

3. **OPTIONS** – what options do you have? What could be your first step? What else could you do? What would you do differently now?

4. **WILL** – what are you going to do? When are you going to do it? On a scale of one to ten, what is the likelihood of success? How do you make it a ten? Who needs to know? What support do you need?

The key skills that the leader–coach needs to display in order to get the best out of this process include the swift building of rapport, never opening a question with a 'why?', intent listening skills (rather than interrupting with 'I did…' or 'When I…', directing and advising), the ability to ask questions that provoke thought/insight and a strong code of confidentiality/ethics. This approach – in combination with the prescribed process – should deliver *clarity* (**g**oal), *awareness* (**r**eality), *choice* (**o**ptions) and *self-belief/motivation* (**w**ill).

Issues

- **The Leader–Coach Dilemma** – in theory, the leader–coach should be able to detach him/herself from prior follower perceptions, biases and prejudices in order to act as a dispassionate, 'uncontaminated' coach; but this is inevitably – given the line manager relationship – hard to achieve. On the plus side, the main benefit of being a leader–coach is that (s)he is (in all probability) in tune with the follower's context and can apply some 'realism filter' to solutions. But the issue for all leader–coaches is that they are often faced by coachees who lack self-awareness (i.e. in Johari window[21] terms, their shortcomings are hidden from themselves but obvious to others). What the leader–coach must try and do is grow self-awareness without infringing – in classic psychotherapeutic terms – into areas that are totally 'blind' to both the coachee and themselves; going beyond normal workplace discourse to solve/address deep-seated psychological issues. In such instances, fully qualified professional therapists should be engaged to help the coachee improve their mental state.

- **The Follower Conundrum** – there is a danger that the subordinate might feel compromised by the process because some of the major blockages to progress actually sit in front of them; namely, their 'leader–coach' line manager! Thus, the follower/recipient might feel that (s)he is merely participating in some elaborate game where ticking the 'process box' in order to please their superior avoids conflict/punishment further on down the line. High levels of trust between both parties are therefore required to make this process work.

---

21 Hase, S., Davies, A., and Dick, B. (1999) The Johari Window and the Dark Side of Organisations, USA: SCU.

How AMs can use this Model

The GROW technique does not need to be formally applied in set-piece engagements. Rather, it is a useful tool that can be applied on a daily basis during brief interactions to get GMs to confront, tackle and solve their own problems. AMs who try and resolve every one of their direct reports' issues are likely, first, to run out of answers (given their distance from day-to-day operations) and, second, to run out of energy. Using the GROW technique helps AMs to devolve responsibility, encourage maturity and increase subordinate self-confidence.

31. GM TRAINING AND DEVELOPMENT FRAMEWORK

Skill Set...	Focus Areas...	Interventions...
TECHNICAL	**Operations/Processes** SOPs, Blueprint, Standards, Legal	Training and testing (OTJ and classroom)
BEHAVIOURAL	**Leadership/Management** Organising, Unit HRM, Coaching, Service	Development and measurement (EOS and 360)
COGNITIVE	**Financial/Marketing** Analytics (diagnosis and prioritisation) and execution/review	Problem solving and simulation, project management

Purpose

The GM (General Manager) Training and Development Framework (TDF) is a simple model that provides a checklist for AMs regarding the training requirements of their direct line reports (and to a certain extent the same for their assistant, deputy and section leaders). It identifies three skill sets (technical, behavioural and cognitive) with specific focus areas, accompanied by key training interventions to accelerate learning. AMs should be mindful of the fact that whilst in-house training programmes are essential for proprietorial knowledge transference (with regards to the particular business's nuances and requirements), any programmes which can offer *accredited, certified qualifications* are likely to have a more profound effect on the learners' willingness to take time out to be developed and their levels of commitment/engagement over the longer term.

Principles and Components

1. *Technical Skills* – these skills are essential for the seamless execution of the FOH and BOH blueprint. They involve the learning of standard operating procedures, standards and legal adherence. These can be trained through in a combination of e-learning (legal compliance testing for instance) and face-to-face (classroom or on-the-job) contexts. This training gives GMs the *explicit* knowledge to do their jobs effectively. Often AMs will use 'the talents' of all their team (including leads, champions, Houses of Excellence etc.) in addition to regional/area trainers in order to bolster technical skills within their team.

2. *Behavioural Skills* – GMs lead teams; the effectiveness of these teams is contingent on their leadership (inspiring and motivating) and management (prioritising, planning and delegating) skills. To some extent, GMs are akin to 'mini-HR' managers – they have to get the best out of their followers through applying effective on-site HRM (communication, development, coaching, performance reviews etc.). Also, as leaders of customer-facing businesses, GMs must be properly trained in service delivery techniques and conflict management. GMs can develop these skills through immersion, observation and development – although it is essential that they fundamentally possess *tacit* 'people personalities'. Often their behavioural skills can be calibrated through regular employee survey feedback, with remedial actions being applied to close gaps in certain areas.

3. *Cognitive Skills* – this part of GM training and development is done notoriously badly by many multi-unit enterprises. Ideally, GMs should be able to problem solve independently through using the qualitative and quantitative insights that flow from their operations. They should have a fair degree of cognitive numeracy: namely, the ability to make analytical connections between the financial and customer outputs of the unit and their operational and staff-related input drivers. Here the AM would be well advised to provide problem-solving workshops and/or be prepared to do intensive one-to-one coaching during business reviews to educate their GMs in 'reading the numbers' and then applying appropriate remedial actions.

Issues

- **Spotting the Gaps** – the TDF assumes that AMs can spot their GM training needs and act accordingly; with targeted development resulting in enhanced unit performance. This is easier said than done. Some GMs (and many humans) are masters at covering up their deficiencies because they don't wish to admit to any weaknesses. The AM must probe deeply to locate gaps, making sure the right interventions are applied for the right deficiencies.

- **Resolving the Gaps** – having located the gaps the AM (as has been stated) must close them. But what if the GM is incapable of making behavioural adjustments or raising their cognitive thinking levels in spite of remedial training? Some attitudes, prejudices, patterns of thinking and processing capabilities are set in stone. The AM can either get the GM to use his team to compensate for some of his/her immutable deficiencies or (in extremis) change the GM.

How AMs can use this Framework

AMs should use this framework as the basis for a skills audit of their team and/or individual direct reports. Gaps that commonly occur across the team can be addressed through intensive group learning. Individual deficiencies should be addressed as part of personal development plans. In all instances, however, the AM only has one outcome in mind: skills training must improve the performance of the district and/or individual units. It is a hard, rather than a soft, tool that is designed to accelerate improvement.

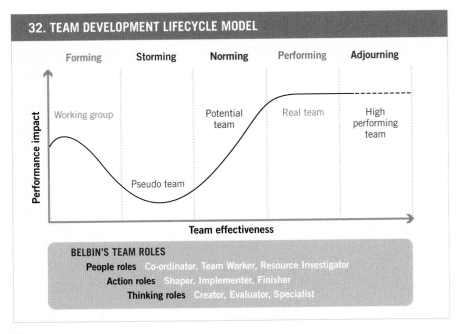

Purpose

The Team Development Lifecycle Model (TDLM)[22] proposes that there are five stages in team development that the managers of teams must

---

22 Adapted from Tuckman, B.W., and Jensen, M. (1977) 'Development Sequences in Small Groups', *Psychological Bulletin of the American Psychological Association*, 63(6).

transition through in order to turn a 'working group' into a 'high-performing team'. Its usefulness for managers stems from its central proposition that teams rarely bond immediately; rather, they transition through a sequential process of development. The quicker the manager can take his/her team through the various stage gates, the faster the team will become a bonded, high-performing unit.

Components and Principles

1. *Dimensions*

   a) *Team Effectiveness* – the extent to which teams form an effective entity over time

   b) *Performance Impact* – the extent to which teams deliver added value outcomes over time

2. *Team Development Stages*

   a) *Stage 1 'Forming'* – at this stage, team working is underdeveloped and managers must determine who fits where. At this stage, the manager will consider the balance of the team (possibly using Belbin's[23] team member archetypes of Shaper, Company Worker, Finisher, Plant, Chairman, Monitor–Evaluator, Resource Investigator, Specialist and Team Worker). At this stage, the team is likely to display signs of self-conscious politeness, embarrassment, over-exuberance/enthusiasm, stilted conversation and limited progress.

   b) *Stage 2 'Storming'* – here the team enters the experimental stage, concerning itself with how it works together. At this point the team displays signs of conflict, lively debate/discussion, 'trying out' and new ways of working. Performance and effectiveness is likely to dip during this 'sorting out' phase.

   c) *Stage 4 'Norming'* – now the team starts to form an identity through shared norms and values (in the case of districts in MUEs, deciding what the team wants to be 'famous for' and what its base values are – 'leave egos outside the door', 'mutual respect', 'togetherness' etc.). During this stage, performance of the team increases.

   d) *Stage 5 'Performing'* – by this stage, relationships within the team are maturing and team members are actively helping one another to achieve goals. At this stage, the team displays signs of a relaxed atmosphere, feelings of confidence, purposeful discussion revolving around goals/tasks and objectives being achieved.

   e) *Stage 5 'Adjourning'* – in this latter period, goals having been achieved, the team (either intentionally or unintentionally) begins to break up and move onto new challenges. At this stage, signs of adjourning

---

23 Belbin, R.M. (1984) *Management Teams: Why They Succeed or Fail*, Oxford: Butterworth Heinemann.

behaviour include: tidying up loose ends, celebrating achievement, feelings of sadness, planning for new teams and saying farewell.

Issues

- **Presumption of Success** – although this model assumes that teams will transition to a high-performing level, in reality many teams will fracture/dissipate at the storming stage. Disputes, egos and self-serving hoarding behaviour (intensified due to stretch budgets, league tables and individualistic incentive programmes) remain unresolved by weak managers or team leaders.
- **Time** – there is no set timeframe for success enfolding this model. Suffice to say that the quicker managers get team members through the storming stage (often through social/relational means: days out, meals, parties etc.) the quicker they perform.

How AMs can use this Model

AMs should be cognisant of and recognise where their team is in terms of development and adapt their approach accordingly. Research has shown that AMs require at least four years of stability on a district to transition through the stages outlined above effectively. Successful AMs accelerate the forming, storming and norming team-development stages to reach a high-performing state faster than their peers.

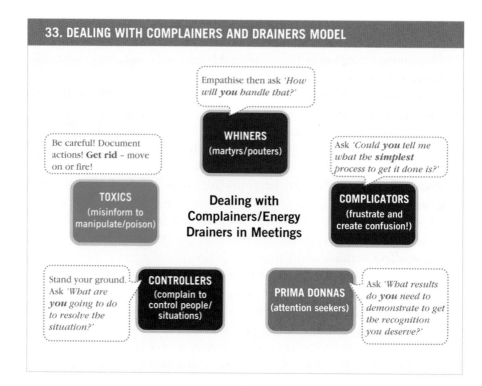

33. DEALING WITH COMPLAINERS AND DRAINERS MODEL

Empathise then ask *'How will you handle that?'*

WHINERS
(martyrs/pouters)

Be careful! Document actions! **Get rid** - move on or fire!

Ask *'Could you tell me what the simplest process to get it done is?'*

TOXICS
(misinform to manipulate/poison)

Dealing with Complainers/Energy Drainers in Meetings

COMPLICATORS
(frustrate and create confusion!)

Stand your ground. Ask *'What are you going to do to resolve the situation?'*

CONTROLLERS
(complain to control people/ situations)

PRIMA DONNAS
(attention seekers)

Ask *'What results do you need to demonstrate to get the recognition you deserve?'*

Purpose

The Dealing with Complainers and Drainers Model is an adaptation of Laura Swindling's[24] excellent book on the subject of coping with tricky personalities who have poor/needy attitudes and behaviours. In a perfect world, the AM's followers will be highly engaged and motivated about the task in hand. The reality is that some of their followers will (for various reasons, such as lack of perspective, immaturity and pure evil!) attempt to derail their attempts to lead the team. Learning techniques to deal with 'Type B' negative characters is a major requirement for AMs as they attempt to engage their wider followership. The major contribution of this model is the suggestion that loaded questions from 'energy sappers' can be despatched and/or diffused by counter questions rather than answers, shifting accountability back to the complainer or drainer.

Principles and Components

There are five categories of complainers and drainers, all of which have idiosyncratic characteristics, requiring tailored approaches:

24 Adapted from Swindling, L. (2013) *Stop Complainers and Energy Drainers: How to Negotiate Work Drama to get More Done*, Hoboken, NJ: J. Wiley & Sons Inc.

1. **Whiners** – these are so-called martyrs and pouters who fail to see the positives in any situation and feel constantly 'done to' and set upon. Constantly whinging about their problems and issues, the AM should counter their questions by firstly empathising with their situation and then shifting accountability by asking 'how will you handle that?'
2. **Complicators** – mendacious types whose sole purpose seems to be to create frustration and confusion by overcomplicating situations ('this won't work because of x, y and z'). AMs should shift accountability by asking 'could you tell me what the simplest process to get it done is?'
3. **Prima Donnas** – these are preening attention seekers who constantly seek praise and validation for their (often) substandard, derisory efforts. AMs should recalibrate their expectations by asking politely 'what results do you need to demonstrate to get the recognition you deserve?'
4. **Controllers** – this cohort uses complaint as its weapon of choice to control people and situations. Their aggressive shop stewardship attracts allies from the disengaged and disenfranchised, helping these so-called controllers shape group dynamics to serve their own purposes. AMs should be brave enough to confront these individuals by, first, acknowledging their sagacious observations and then, second, asking
5. **Toxics** – these are the worst of the lot: dissembling types who deliberately misinform (either through gossip or rumour mongering) in order to manipulate and poison the minds of others. AMs should handle this type with care – they usually possess feral intelligence! AMs must document their actions with, and observation of, these individuals as supportive evidence for when the day comes either to fire them or to move them on.

Issues

- **Discriminating between Types** – one of the difficulties faced by the AM is deciding which *principal* category some of their complaining/draining types fall into and, consequently, which tack they should take with each individual. Some complainers will display all of the attributes listed above. However, whilst some categories are slightly blurred and overlapping, there is one that will be important to locate as quickly as possible in order to neutralise its destructive effects: the toxics.
- **The Good Guys** – this model, whilst realistic, is slightly depressing. What about the good guys? The first thing to say is that there will be many 'Type A' positive personalities on the district who will ameliorate the effect of these complainers and drainers. Second, as the AM increases his/her stock of the good guys, behaviours within the group will become more self-regulating, with some of the good guys calling complainers

and drainers to account for their poor attitudes/behaviours, which they (rightfully) claim to be 'holding everyone else back'.

How AMs can use this Model

AMs can use this model to spot and nullify the impact of complainers and drainers within their team. There is one generic category-killing question that will silence many of these types, which the AM can usefully deploy against these mood killers: namely, 'what an interesting question. Can you research some solutions to the problem you've raised and present your findings back to the team at the next district meeting?'

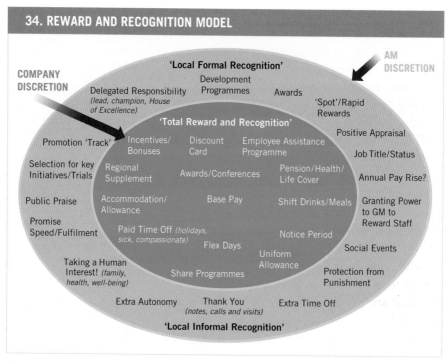

Purpose

The Reward and Recognition Model (RRM) illustrates two layers of reward and recognition in MUEs, one determined by company policy and the other (sub-divided into local formal/informal categories) which can be driven by AM discretion. What it seeks to demonstrate is that the AM has an array of tools at his/her disposal to animate subordinates!

Components and Principles

1. *Company Discretion* – at the centre of the RRM lie the company's total reward and recognition practices including important hygiene factors such as its base pay parameters and benefits package.

2. *AM Discretion*

    a) *Local Formal Recognition* – AMs have a bundle of recognition tools (some derived from the company level) that they can deploy at district, unit or individual level to motivate their team/subordinates. These are usually tangible and visible.

    b) *Local Informal Recognition* – less formal, more intangible – but nonetheless just as important – AMs use *currencies of exchange* with followers that build subordinate emotional bank accounts which they can 'draw down' at various junctures. Indeed, such behaviour is likely to generate reciprocity and *indebtedness* from recipients resulting in enhanced exchanges of discretionary effort, loyalty and engagement which helps facilitate the AM to achieve operational excellence and organic growth without direct daily supervision.

Issues

- **Favouritism** – AMs must use formal and informal reward/recognition devices to signal approval for real performance outcomes rather than using them as forms of 'soft patronage' for favourites.
- **Carrot and Stick** – the RRM highlights the carrots that AMs can use to co-opt followers psychologically; but in some instances the stick (i.e. more coercive methods) will be required for the recalcitrant and the workshy.

How AMs can use this Model

AMs should review the reward and recognition toolkit at their disposal and, prior to deployment, make sure this fits with the behaviours they want to stimulate from certain individuals (i.e. match what will be valued by the recipient and will result in higher performance levels). For instance, 'Star' GMs will most likely value development/progression opportunities whilst 'Pillar' GMs might value responsibility, autonomy, protection from punishment or a heartfelt thank you more highly.

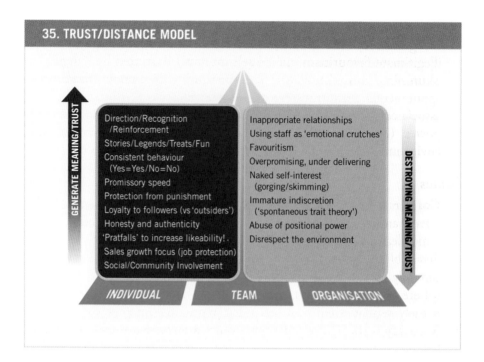

35. TRUST/DISTANCE MODEL

GENERATE MEANING/TRUST

Direction/Recognition
/Reinforcement
Stories/Legends/Treats/Fun
Consistent behaviour
(Yes=Yes/No=No)
Promissory speed
Protection from punishment
Loyalty to followers (vs 'outsiders')
Honesty and authenticity
'Pratfalls' to increase likeability!.
Sales growth focus (job protection)
Social/Community Involvement

Inappropriate relationships
Using staff as 'emotional crutches'
Favouritism
Overpromising, under delivering
Naked self-interest
(gorging/skimming)
Immature indiscretion
('spontaneous trait theory')
Abuse of positional power
Disrespect the environment

DESTROYING MEANING/TRUST

INDIVIDUAL   TEAM   ORGANISATION

Purpose

Building trust is crucial in human relations and is generally portrayed as the extent to which one party believes that another party will act both transparently and consistently in a fair/benevolent manner. The Trust-Distance Model (T-DM) – which illustrates how AMs generate trust – includes some elements of the previous RRM, but also incorporates some important references as to how trust relations are undermined.

Components and Principles

1. *Dimensions* – trust operates at an organisational, team and individual level. Psychological distance between managers and followers is either closed down or opened up according to whether or not high or low levels of trust exist.

2. *Qualifiers for Trust* – these include factors such as a clear direction (pursued with a constancy of purpose), recognition of good performance, the dissemination of positive stories/legends, consistent adjudication/behaviour, quickly following up on promises, protecting followers from unwarranted punishment (because the law is an ass or there are insufficient resources), displaying follower loyalty to 'outsiders', honest/authentic behaviour, pratfalls which demonstrate human fallibility, an unwavering commitment to business growth (signalling a commitment to job protection/security) and a genuine interest in social cohesion.

3. *Destroyers of Trust* – include factors such as inappropriate relationships, using subordinates as emotional crutches (looking for sympathy), illegitimate favouritism, naked self-interest (illustrated by 'gorging' or 'skimming' on the district), immature indiscretion (leading to spontaneous trait transference, where negative sentiments become associated with the character of the tell-tale), exploitation of positional power (manifested through bullying and unjust coercion) and environmental disrespect (a major turn off for Gen Y workers).

Issues

- **Corporate Derailment** – whilst the AM might act in a trustworthy, open-handed and honest manner in their follower interactions, their senior leadership cadre might constantly derail their position through dissembling rhetoric and behaviours. AMs faced with this conundrum can only do one thing: accept that corporate behaviour lies outside their sphere of influence – all they can do is 'control their controllables', namely regulate their own behaviour, reputation and disposition.
- **Recovery** – the T-DM infers that once trust is lost, it has disappeared forever; however, genuine mea culpas and admissions of wrongdoing will be accepted if there are no further misdemeanours or slip ups. AMs would do well to beware of the 'jungle bush telegraph': don't try and cover up, you will be found out in the end!

How AMs can use this Model

AMs should examine the T-DM and ask themselves whether they are increasing or reducing psychological distance with their followers through either trust-inducing or trust-eroding behaviour. Self-serving, expedient behaviour on the part of the AM might produce some short-term gains but ultimately the AM's poor reputation will result in a migration of talent and a lack of internal/external succession. With regard to formal communications – a major signal of behaviour – AMs should ask themselves the following questions:

- Process – am I communicating through the right channels to 'get to' my team and followers? (Am I over-reliant on email as opposed to social media and face-to-face?)
- Content – is the content of my communications (particularly weekly end-of-business summaries) fair and balanced? Does it praise both absolute and relative performance/progress? Does it name and shame (through league tableitis) or build and grow (remember, positive comments should outnumber critical ones by a factor of 5:1 to maintain motivation)? Are my messages consistent and mature?

SECTION 3

EXECUTE

Blueprint and Plan

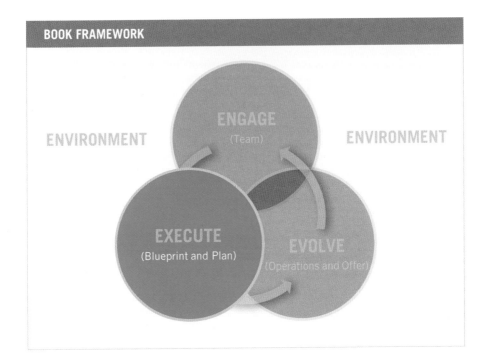

BOOK FRAMEWORK

ENVIRONMENT

ENGAGE
(Team)

ENVIRONMENT

EXECUTE
(Blueprint and Plan)

EVOLVE
(Operations and Offer)

Execution is eased through the process of engagement. Once Area Managers have engaged their followers, they must drive operational excellence and organic growth through executing the brand blueprint and the financial plan. The models in this section help Area Managers understand the core concepts and processes underpinning seamless execution.

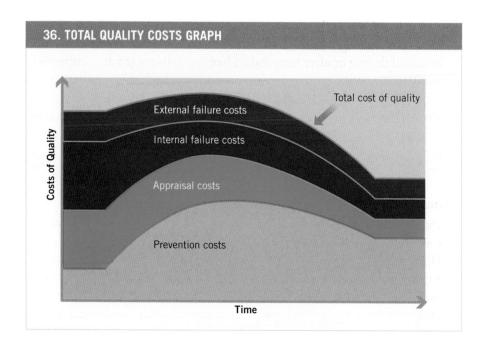

36. TOTAL QUALITY COSTS GRAPH

Total cost of quality

Costs of Quality

External failure costs

Internal failure costs

Appraisal costs

Prevention costs

Time

Purpose

The Total Quality Costs Graph (TQCG)[25] illustrates how increasing the resources devoted to quality preservation (through selection, immersion, training, ongoing total quality management programmes etc.) has a positive long-term correlation with reducing the overall costs associated with quality breakdowns. The TQCG demonstrates how the costs of ensuring quality in a typical business rise initially as investment in proactive prevention increases. However, having shifted emphasis from a reactive 'inspection regime' to a 'right first time' approach, total quality costs decrease over time.

Components and Principles

There are four categories of quality-related costs in this model which, added together, form the total costs of quality in a standard business:

1. ***External Failure Costs*** – these are costs associated with errors being experienced by customers (costs = decline in customer satisfaction, time resolving complaints, legal costs and costs associated with returns/refunds).

2. ***Internal Failure Costs*** – failure costs connected with errors that require constant resolution within the organisation (costs = time and cost of rectification, reworks, wastage, lost productivity and wasted trouble-shooting effort).

---

25 Adapted from Slack, N., Chambers, S., and Johnston, R. (2008) *Operations and Process Management: Principles and Practice for Strategic Impact*, Financial Times/Prentice Hall.

3. *Appraisal Costs* – these are auditing/checking costs, usually associated with controlling quality; checking whether problems/errors have occurred during or after the product/service delivery (costs = inspection, audit and compliance personnel, time spent checking/monitoring and producing reports for remedial action).
4. *Prevention Costs* – operator costs incurred in 'getting it right first time' (costs = initial service/product/process design, time/resources spent hiring quality people, extensive immersion/training and on-site TQM systems).

Issues

- **Defective Product/Service** – the TQCG essentially argues that 'on the spot' operator investment will – in time – reduce total quality costs. However, one major contaminant variable that (in spite of the efforts of engaged frontline operatives) will constantly undermine prevention efforts is a defective product and/or service concept. Policy makers and designers must ensure that process clarity/simplicity and resilience are built in during initial stages.
- **Visibility of Prevention Costs** – according to Henry Ford 'quality means doing it right when no-one is looking!' – implying that ultimately (and especially in dispersed multi-unit contexts) bringing down the total costs of quality is contingent upon the diligence and discretionary effort of operators who care. To this extent, costly central/local HRM systems that engage/motivate operators are important; the problem is, however, their cost visibility to senior policy makers compared other 'invisible' expenses (such as checking, monitoring and reworks) meaning they are more susceptible to cuts.

How AMs can use this Model

Looking at the four categories of the costs of quality, estimate how much an increased investment and 'doing it right first time' (quality local HRM) will reduce the costs of appraisal (inspection/audits/checks), internal failure (rectification/wastage) and external failure (customer dissatisfaction and a decline in item purchases/visit frequency) leading to an overall drop in costs associated with quality. In short, putting the right people in place, with the right attitudes and skills, will dramatically decrease costs associated with inspection and quality breakdowns!

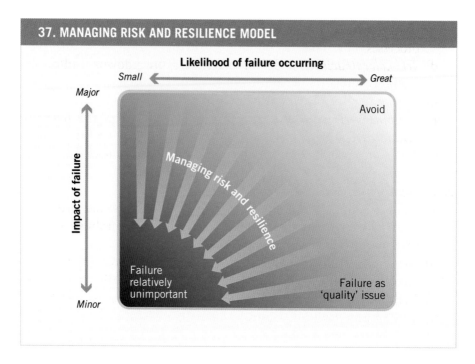

37. MANAGING RISK AND RESILIENCE MODEL

Likelihood of failure occurring

Small ← → Great

Major

Impact of failure

Avoid

Managing risk and resilience

Failure relatively unimportant

Failure as 'quality' issue

Minor

Purpose

Risk represents the potential for undesirable failure from some 'event', whilst resilience is an organisation's realisable capability to stop and/or recover from these events. The Managing Risk and Resilience Model[26] (MRRM) conceives of managers and organisations being able to highlight/scope the risk of failures in relation to their importance and then, subsequently, improve resilience by minimising their impact and/or chance of occurrence in order to preserve their reputation/levels of performance.

Components and Principles

Most organisations clearly wish to minimise any major risks (those represented by the top right-hand corner of the MRRM: high importance and likelihood of occurring). But what are the potential causes of failure and how can they be minimised?

1. *Potential Causes of Failure*
   a) *Supply Chain* – particularly in 'lean just-in-time' systems
   b) *Human* – especially in dispersed multi-site organisations (due to a lack of direct daily supervision/control)

---

26 Adapted from Slack, N., Chambers, S., and Johnston, R. (2008) *Operations and Process Management: Principles and Practice for Strategic Impact*, Financial Times/Prentice Hall.

c) *Organisational* – inappropriate design of structures, policies and processes
d) *Technology/Facilities* – IT or machinery breakdowns and/or site malfunctions
e) *Product/Service* – lack of testing/piloting/remodelling
f) *Customer* – misuse or abuse of products (through the so-called 'sovereign' effect and/or a lack of customer competency)
g) *Environmental* – legal, legislative or external 'acts of god'

2. **Estimating the Likelihood of Failure**
   a) *Objective estimates* – failure rates ('how often?') and reliability (chances of occurrence); both estimates can help robust scenario planning, stress testing and contingency planning
   b) *Subjective* – going beyond the knowns to imagining the unimaginable i.e. left-field showstoppers that could completely derail the operation (for instance, 'casino' market bets and unforeseen regulatory intervention in large industrial concerns).

Issues

- **Hidden risks** – organisations are notoriously bad at risk assessing the unintended consequences of some of their decisions (particularly when senior policy-makers lack operational tacit knowledge). Measuring risk and building in resilience is an art and science; there are the Rumsfeldian knowns, known unknowns and unknown unknowns.
- **False Resilience** – in some cultures, operators will claim that systems and processes are resilient enough to withstand/minimise certain risks. The degree to which people are willing to be honest and blow the whistle on contraventions is dependent on culturally related levels of collectivism and self-protection that lead to covering up and/or face-saving behaviours.

How AMs can use this Model

Populate the MRRM with the risks of failure that threaten to derail your businesses (i.e. hygiene, theft, injury, slacking etc.). Taking into account their level of likelihood and potential impact costs, how do you increase the resilience of your businesses?

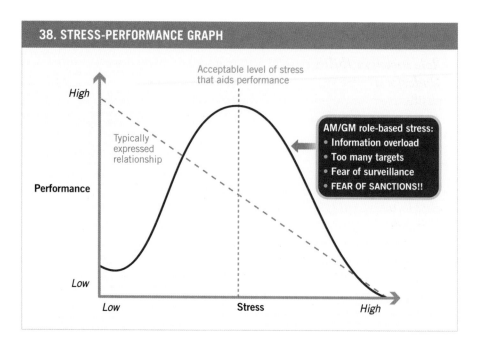

38. STRESS-PERFORMANCE GRAPH

Acceptable level of stress that aids performance

High

Performance

Typically expressed relationship

AM/GM role-based stress:
• Information overload
• Too many targets
• Fear of surveillance
• FEAR OF SANCTIONS!!

Low

Low   Stress   High

Purpose

The Stress-Performance Curve Graph[27] (SPCG) illustrates how a moderate amount of stress can actually aid performance for managers, whilst excessively high or low levels can debilitate performance. This model offers a contrarian approach to other stress-related models that assume a 'straight-line' relationship between stress and performance. The SPCG also helps categorise/identify the main stressors that tip managers from moderate levels of stress (and high performance) into a state of high stress (which hampers performance).

Components and Principles

The underlying hypothesis of this model is that high and low stress levels derail performance whilst moderate amounts of stress aid high performance. But what are the main managerial stressors?

1. *Overload* – inordinate number of tasks due to central demands and covering for shirkers (lazy supervisors, peers and subordinates)
2. *Conflict* – toxic relations with others (supervisors, peers and subordinates)
3. *Stretch Targets* – unreachable stretch targets (missing them gives rise to

---

27 Adapted from Dawson, T. (2000) *Principles and Practice of Modern Management*, Liverpool Academic Press.

the threat of punishment) backed up by highly visible surveillance-based league tables

4. *Role Incompatibility* – lack of will or skill to do the role
5. *Underload* – too little to do, resulting in boredom and/or fear for job position

Issues

- **Stressor Resolution** – for those managers in the middle of the organisation (facing competing and irreconcilable demands from the frontline and the strategic apex), a lack of purposeful action by policy makers (say on stretch targets) means that certain stressors will persist for a long duration. In these circumstances, operator–managers must consider what *relative* success looks like within their controllable universe (such as strong year-on-year performance rather than performance against budget).
- **Psychological Predisposition** – some individuals (through conditioning and/or personality) can be laid-back or highly strung. Achieving the mid-point of stress (which results in optimal performance outcomes) will be a challenge for both ends of the spectrum.

How AMs can use this Model

AMs should consider where their level of stress lies (low, moderate or high); ask peers, friends and family. Ask yourself what your main stressors are and how they can be controlled or held at a moderate level. Gain a sense of perspective ('what's the worst that can happen to me in this situation?') and use some of the analysis, planning and implementation tools from this chapter to reduce your number of stressors.

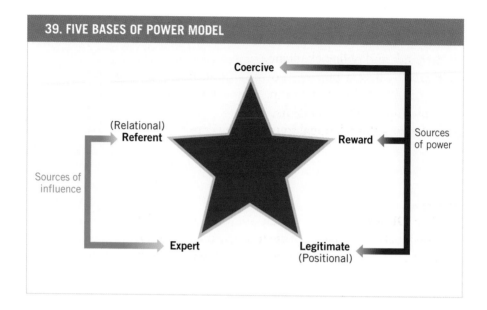

39. FIVE BASES OF POWER MODEL

Coercive

(Relational)
Referent

Reward

Sources
of power

Sources of
influence

Expert

Legitimate
(Positional)

Purpose

The Five Bases of Power Model was conceived by social psychologists French and Raven[28] to articulate the five distinct 'bases' of authority possessed by humans during their interactions with others. Understanding which bases fit which situations enables individuals to expedite their own personal agendas and objectives effectively.

Principles and Components

This model identifies five main power sources available to humans (although a sixth – informational power, the ability to bring about change through 'information resources' – was added later):

1. *Coercive* – this source of power is derived from a person's ability to utilise the threat of force and punishment in order to coerce other individuals to comply with their demands.

2. *Reward* – this base of power is derived from an individual's capacity to compensate others for compliance with their objectives, either tangibly (i.e. monetarily) or intangibly (i.e. socio-emotional recognition). However, the rewards that are exchanged must be of sufficiently high perceived value by the recipient for them to guide purposeful behavioural outcomes.

3. *Legitimate* – this power source comes from an understanding and belief

28 Adapted from French, J., and Raven, B. (1959) 'The Bases of Social Power' in D. Cartwright, *Studies in Social Power*, Ann Arbor, MI: Institute for Social Research, pp.150–167.

amongst others that a person has assigned formal authority (principally due to their dominant positional status within the hierarchy) to make demands and oblige obedience.

4. *Expert* – here a person's power and authority is derived from their credibility within the group, connected to their perceived superior knowledge, skills and talents.

5. *Referent* – this relational source of power refers to high levels of personal likability, worthiness and charm resulting in bonding affiliation and attachment responses from others.

Issues

- **One Dimensional** – French and Raven's framework assumes that individuals can make recourse to singular bases of power in order to fulfil their objectives. The reality is that power is multi-dimensional and various aspects of their bases need to be used at various times to fit with circumstances (based on a person's capability and situational/follower needs).

- **Cultural Effects** – points of power suggests that individuals have options and choices regarding their adopted power source. The reality is that in some cultures certain power resources are more preferred than others; namely, coercion is favoured in some societies compared to others.

How AMs can use this Model

AMs should ask themselves the following:
- What are my main power sources?
- What base of power is likely to result in effective compliance amongst my followers, peers or wider stakeholders?
- Should I adopt a universal (one size fits all) approach to exercising power, or adapt my style to individual needs?

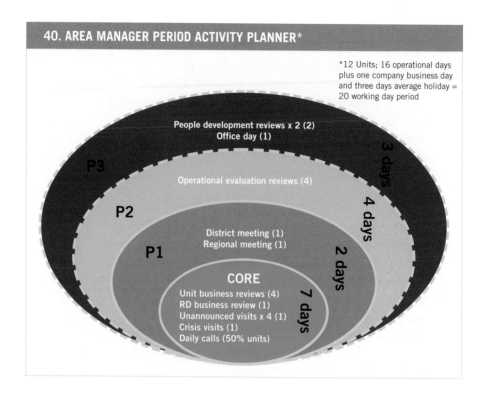

40. AREA MANAGER PERIOD ACTIVITY PLANNER*

*12 Units; 16 operational days plus one company business day and three days average holiday = 20 working day period

People development reviews x 2 (2)
Office day (1)

P3

3 days

Operational evaluation reviews (4)

P2

4 days

District meeting (1)
Regional meeting (1)

P1

2 days

CORE
Unit business reviews (4)
RD business review (1)
Unannounced visits x 4 (1)
Crisis visits (1)
Daily calls (50% units)

7 days

Purpose

The Area Manager Period Activity Planner (PAP) is an indicative model of the general routine that MUE firms expect their AMs to follow in a four-week business period (i.e. thirteen cycles in any given year). Activities are subdivided into priority order. Some are mandatory and must be completed by the AM themselves – others with lower priority ranking can be completed by colleagues (i.e. such as the AM's 'buddy' or senior GMs in the district). PAPs are designed to give a shape and coherence to the role, whilst ensuring that a robust communications cascade system is in place for the organisation to transmit/transfer vital information and updates.

Principles and Components

This PAP (based upon 12 stores/units) envisages four zones of activity covering 16 operational days within the period business cycle (the other three being designated as leave and one day as a company business day: training, conferences etc.):

1. **Core** – these activities must be completed every period even if the AM takes a couple of weeks holiday and should be executed by the AM personally:

a) *Unit Business Reviews* – a full P&L and diagnostic analysis of the unit's historic performance and forward plan (4 days per period = 12 days per quarter; to cover whole district)

b) *Regional Director Business Review* – a full P&L and diagnostic analysis of the district with the Area Manager's line manager (1 day per period)

c) *Unannounced Visits* – unannounced visits to check on a *specific* aspect of operational execution (4 targeted visits per period, totalling 1 day = 100%+ district coverage during quarter)

d) *Crisis Visits* – this is a contingency day reserved for extreme emergencies such as legal issues, health and safety, disciplinaries etc. (1 day per period)

e) *Daily Calls* – the AM must make telephone contact with, or digitally 'facetime', 50% of their units a day (achieving 100% coverage every 2 days). On Mondays, the AM should hold a one-hour conference/video call against a set agenda (review dashboard performance, review league table performance, updates on key focus areas, initiatives and projects etc.).

2. ***Priority 1 (P1)*** – these activities must be executed every period but can be covered by nominated substitutes (AM's buddy and/or lead/champion GMs):

a) *Regional Meeting* – review of performance and schedule of initiatives; attendees include regional director, AMs and invitees from support functions (1 day per period)

b) *District Meeting* – consistent meeting structure built around signature purpose and KPIs; short review of the past – majority of items are forward looking (1 day per period *after* the regional meeting).

3. ***Priority 2 (P2)*** – this activity must happen every period but does not have to covered when the AM is on holiday:

Operational Evaluation Reviews – these are planned audits of operational blueprint compliance (4 days per period = 12 days per quarter; to cover whole district).

4. ***Priority 3 (P3)*** – same as P2 but with less of a planning priority;

a) *People Development Reviews* – personal development plan and HR reviews (2 days – 2 PDRs per day = 100% district coverage per period)

b) *Office Day* – Period/Quarterly planning and scheduling day 'at home' (1 day per period).

Issues

- **Realism** – the PAP is a standard tool used by most MUEs to ensure consistency and uniformity of activity amongst their AM populations. The reality is that, often, this perfect symmetry of pre-designated activity is derailed by unanticipated events and/or urgent central diktats that 'crash the diary'. An allowance of only one day for crises is – in some organisational contexts – slightly optimistic. In addition, given the variation in performance between the AM's units, it is unlikely that the balance of their time will be sub-divided equally. In order to turnaround or re-boot underperforming units, the AM is likely to devote more time to the 'laggards' (who represent real P&L upside) rather than the 'outperformers'; although (s)he must be careful not to neglect the GMs/teams that are doing well.
- **Lack of People Focus** – what stands out in most PAPs is the priority weighting accorded to business planning reviews ('Core') in comparison to people development reviews (Priority 3). AMs must therefore maximise every opportunity in all interactions with their GMs and teams to check upon talent attraction and development rather than waiting for these set-piece opportunities.

How AMs can use this Model

This model is a rather prescriptive representation of what the AM should execute on a quarterly basis – assuming virtual equanimity between units. However, it does provide a useful checklist of activities. Looking at this framework, AMs should ask themselves:

- Have I scheduled in sufficient time with my units to cover all or some of these vital activities?
- Have I got a covering AM buddy and/or dependable lead/champion GMs who can substitute for me on certain key occasions?

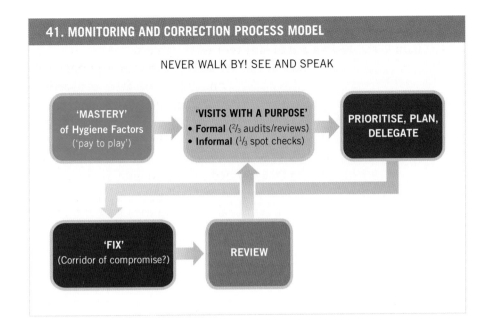

41. MONITORING AND CORRECTION PROCESS MODEL

NEVER WALK BY! SEE AND SPEAK

'MASTERY' of Hygiene Factors ('pay to play')

'VISITS WITH A PURPOSE'
• **Formal** ($^{2}/_{3}$ audits/reviews)
• **Informal** ($^{1}/_{3}$ spot checks)

PRIORITISE, PLAN, DELEGATE

'FIX' (Corridor of compromise?)

REVIEW

Purpose

The Monitoring and Correction Process Model (MCPM) illustrates how AMs should protect the reputation of the brand through checks (both planned and ad hoc), action plans and follow up. This process underpins standards and operational excellence reviews – a fundamental element of maintaining the consistency, uniformity and quality of a product/service. In franchising, this monitoring process is designed to prevent poor system operators freeloading within the network, shirking their responsibility to maintain a high-quality product/service.

Components and Principles

This sequential process model has the following elements:

1. *Mastery* – the AM needs to understand the key interlocking elements of the blueprint (both BOH/FOH). In most organisations, (s)he will be guided during formal visits by operational excellence review checklists and documentation. However, in informal visits where the AM conducts spot checks, (s)he will require both explicit and tacit knowledge of minimum standards requirements and potential breaches.

2. *'Visits with a Purpose'* – these can be sub-divided into 'formal' and 'informal':

   a) *Formal* – these are pre-scheduled visits conducted either by the AM, audit team or peers. A thorough review of operational standards is conducted, resulting in an overall compliance score coupled with a remedial actions list. 'Show stopping' breaches (e.g. food hygiene in hospitality) might result in a zero rating!

b) *Informal* – one-third of all visits should be informal and ad hoc to test compliance in 'real time' operations. Here the AM might target a particular point of known/suspected weakness in the operation, derived from analysis of unit data on customer satisfaction surveys, for instance.

3. ***Prioritise, Plan and Delegate*** – following these visits, remedial actions should be detailed for action in priority order (according to 'costs of quality' and risk impact), a plan to address the breakdowns should be jointly agreed and their implementation should be delegated out to nominated unit personnel and/or support functions.

4. ***'Fix'*** – fixes should be applied swiftly in accordance with the plan, appropriate resources having been mobilised/supervised by the GM.

5. ***Review*** – remedial actions should be reviewed with (as the MCPM illustrates) further visits with a purpose. If defective elements remain, further plans should be drawn up for expediting etc.

Issues

- **Monitoring Costs** – costs of blueprint monitoring in MUEs can be high but (as previous models have demonstrated – see TQCG) they can be reduced if sufficient prevention mechanisms (such as having enough trained staff who care) are put in place at the outset. Often, standards/compliance breakdowns are symptomatic of poor management – their root cause can be resolved by addressing core underlying issues rather than just resolving the breakdown itself.

- **Compliance Cultures** – in certain cultures, 100% compliance to the blueprint is required/demanded. However, in some circumstances – due to resource starvation and/or opaque guidance – this demand is unrealistic and untenable. In this context, the AM therefore needs to use some discretion (the so called 'circle of compromise') with regards to what 'must' be done versus the 'nice to haves', holding back severe coercive/punitive action due to an understanding of the situation.

How AMs can use this Model

The MCPM is essentially a checklist and sense-making tool which AMs can use to address the following questions:
- Do I have sufficient mastery of the blueprint?
- Do I know what I am looking for during ad hoc/informal visits with a purpose? (Is my visit driven by data insights or is it just a random 'turn up and check'?)

- Am I using all the resources on my district/support services to assist in providing swift remedial action for serious breaches? (Training, qualified personnel, 'fixes' etc.)
- Do I 'give my GMs the pen' during visits so they can 'mark the unit'? (This will build accountability and insight!)
- Do I give more praise for catching them doing it right than admonishment for getting it wrong?

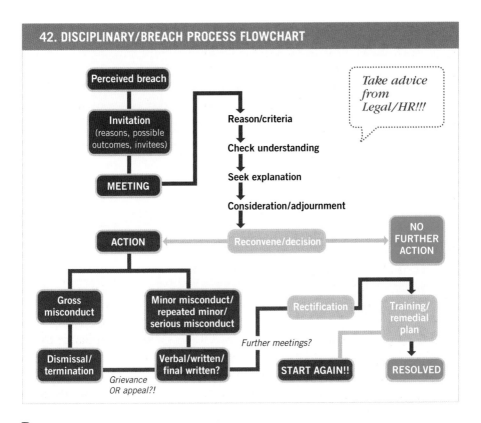

Purpose

The Disciplinary/Breach Process Flowchart (DBFC) highlights the procedural steps that AMs must transition through if they intend to take formal disciplinary action for serious breaches of company policy. Failure to follow procedure is the most common reason why disciplinary actions fail or result in large claims for compensation (often on the grounds of constructive dismissal). It must be stressed that this route must be used as a last resort: regular usage by AMs will create a climate of fear in their districts and (in some instances) have a paralysing effect on performance.

Components and Principles

The *main* sub-components of this flowchart are as follows:

1. *Invitation* – write to the recipient inviting them to a meeting, clearly stating the subject matter, its possible outcomes and (if necessary) allowance for accompanying representatives.
2. *Reason/Criteria* – at the meeting, clearly state the breach of company policy and/or area of underperformance against agreed criteria (state that minutes of the meeting will be taken).
3. *Check Understanding* – check recipient understanding of the breach and the rules/procedures.
4. *Explanation* – seek an explanation for the breach (take detailed minutes).
5. *Consideration* – take time out to give serious consideration to the explanation and actions to be taken (if a satisfactory explanation is given, no further action is to be taken).
6. *Reconvene Meeting* – give the recipient the adjudication outcome and its reasons.
7. *Issue Formal Warning* – issue formal warning (verbal or written), state length of time on file and appeals procedure.
8. *Rectification* – jointly agree a measurable improvement plan with associated training/guidance and future meeting dates.

Issues

- **Overuse** – given the multiplicity of policies, practices and measures coupled with (in some cases) a lack of resources that junior and middle managers have access to in MUEs, there are bound to be multiple breaches of the letter of the law. Overzealous AMs that resort to using this corrective route will create a climate of fear in their districts which will – most likely – stymie discretionary effort and innovative behaviours. This coercive path should be used sparingly and judiciously.
- **Procedural Non-adherence** – if this procedure is badly handled it could result in an internal grievance being launched by the recipient or (in the case of dismissal) a tribunal appeal. AMs who trigger this course of action must always ask themselves whether their case will be water-tight in such forums. Trigger happy AMs who discipline subordinates 'on a whim' (often to frighten them in order to move them out of units) should consider the potential financial and reputational costs to the company of fabricating cases or junking procedure.

How AMs can use this Process

AMs should always consult with their line manager and HR personnel before embarking on this process to 'sense check' that, first, their action is warranted and, second, they are going to follow the appropriate steps. However, AMs who frequently resort to this process as a means of performance management need to understand that it will be a lengthy, attritional process. AMs with high levels of nous and guile rarely utilise formal disciplinary processes as they are masters at sorting out issues through informal, off-the-record 'car-park chats' where they read serious transgressors their 'horoscopes', managing poor performers out in a far more covert but effective manner.

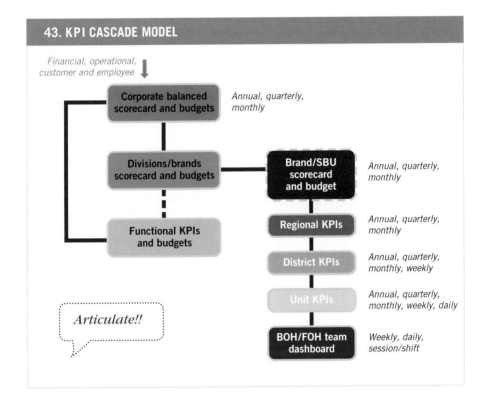

43. KPI CASCADE MODEL

Purpose
The KPI Cascade Model (KPICM) illustrates how targets/measures flow from the strategic apex to the operational point of impact within MUEs. It exists to ensure alignment, line of sight and coherence of purpose from top to bottom in dispersed multi-site operations.

Components and Principles
The KPICM shows a hierarchical cascade of core objectives/targets, with best-practice companies having designed top-level targets with a deep

understanding of the prime drivers at the customer level within the organisation/brand. Functions will have their own enabling KPIs whilst the operational line will have a 'multi-layered net' of KPIs:

1. **Corporate Balanced Scorecard/Budget** – these will generally incorporate financial and customer outputs, combined with people and operational process inputs (see the Balanced Scorecard Model). These will fit with the top-line corporate strategy.

2. **Divisional/Brand Scorecard/Budget** – this will mirror the corporate scorecard albeit targets will be proportionately adjusted for (in multi-brand operations) the business model (sales, margins, fixed/variable costs), investment plans etc.

3. **Functional KPIs/Budgets** – incorporate enabling KPIs which have discreet targets (i.e. supply chain – purchasing spend variance, marketing – promotional ROI, HR – staff stability/turnover %, property – defect resolution times and 'new build to budget').

4. **Operational Line**
   a) *Regional KPIs* – financial, customer, operational and people (annual, quarterly and monthly targets)
   b) *District KPIs* – same KPIs as region (annual, quarterly, monthly and weekly targets)
   c) *Unit KPIs* – same KPIs as district (incorporate daily targets)
   d) *BOH/FOH Team Dashboards* – unit KPIs broken down into shift and session targets.

Issues

- **Articulation** – very often in MUEs, KPIs stop at unit level and their execution is hampered by a lack of articulation at team, session and shift level. AMs and GMs must break down 'macro' monthly/weekly KPIs into 'micro' daily objectives (such as numbers of meals sold per shift within hospitality or items sold in retail) to, first, bring the KPI targets alive and, second, focus on deliverables which will address seemingly detached/distant macro-targets.

- **Stretch Targets** – ideal MUEs might have elaborate KPI cascade and associated incentive mechanisms in place to stimulate the correct behaviours/outcomes but their efforts will count for nothing if the stretch targets themselves are perceived as unrealistic and unattainable. Indeed, they can have the opposite effect of that intended – destabilising rather than motivating teams to achieve high performance levels.

- **Communications** – preferably organisations will explain the 'why' behind the KPIs in order to achieve buy-in. Often KPIs (and especially budgets) are imposed top-down, well into the financial year, with teams having had little preparation to get a fast start – a state of affairs that can foster disillusionment and apathy.

How AMs can use this Model

AMs should ask themselves whether important unit KPIs are, first, understood and bought into by the whole team and, second, check that they are properly articulated to guide performance-driven behaviours and actions on a daily, session and shift basis.

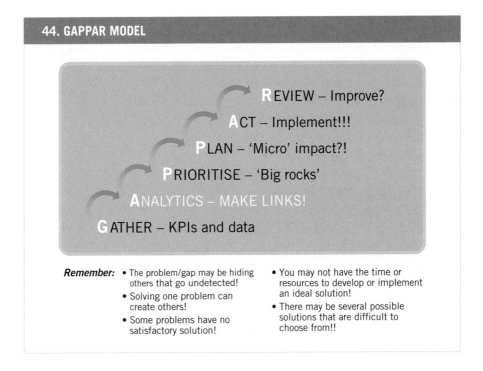

44. GAPPAR MODEL

REVIEW – Improve?

ACT – Implement!!!

PLAN – 'Micro' impact?!

PRIORITISE – 'Big rocks'

ANALYTICS – MAKE LINKS!

GATHER – KPIs and data

Remember:
- The problem/gap may be hiding others that go undetected!
- Solving one problem can create others!
- Some problems have no satisfactory solution!

- You may not have the time or resources to develop or implement an ideal solution!
- There may be several possible solutions that are difficult to choose from!!

Purpose

The GAPPAR Model is an 'acronymed' sequential process model which highlights the stages AMs should transition through to close the gap on either KPI underperformance or resolving operational malfunctions.

Components and Principles

The GAPPAR process runs as follows:
1. *Gather* – assemble all key organisational performance objectives.
2. *Analytics* – conduct GAP analysis of portfolio/unit performance against KPI objectives and blueprint (benchmark against best/worst within the district, company and – where possible – competitors). Most importantly,

analytically make the linkages and connections between inputs/outputs and discriminate between symptoms/root causes.

3. *Prioritise* – identify the 'big rocks' that will accelerate performance. According to the Pareto principle, 80% of most problems in organisations will be rooted in 20% of the operation! Locate these 'rocks' that will have a disproportionate improvement effects and drive their solution relentlessly.

4. *Plan* – formulate plans: by whom, by when? ENSURE METRICS AND KPIs ARE MICRO TRANSLATED/CASCADED TO COLLEAGUES/ TEAM MEMBERS

5. *Act* – drive implementation, whilst telling others about the plan and benefits (including peers, support staff and superiors): this increases the likelihood of it becoming a self-fulfilling prophecy.

6. *Review* – measure performance outcomes; incrementally improve.

Issues

- **Art and Science** – the process of analysis, diagnosis, prioritisation and rectification is not straightforward. The AM will have to apply his/her explicit and tacit knowledge of operations to unscramble issues (both quantitatively and qualitatively) to make dependable linkages that result in plans that produce tangible problem resolution – otherwise, a lot of time and effort will be wasted tackling issues with miss-matched solutions.

- **Conundrums** – AMs would do well to be aware that the problem/gap they are attempting to rectify might be hiding others that have gone undetected. Solving one problem might unintentionally cause others. Moreover, some problems actually have no satisfactory solution and AMs will often lack the time/resources for complete resolution. In some instances, they will have several solutions that will be difficult to discriminate between in terms of net outcomes/effectiveness.

How AMs can use this Model

GAPPAR is a useful problem-resolution checklist for the AM – the models following GAPPAR are more analytical, providing further insight into how AMs locate vital insights/connections, prioritise 'big rock' actions and effectively implement remedial actions.

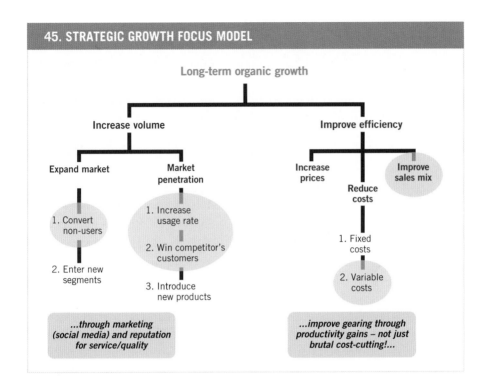

45. STRATEGIC GROWTH FOCUS MODEL

Long-term organic growth

Increase volume

- Expand market
  1. Convert non-users
  2. Enter new segments

- Market penetration
  1. Increase usage rate
  2. Win competitor's customers
  3. Introduce new products

...through marketing (social media) and reputation for service/quality

Improve efficiency

- Increase prices
- Reduce costs
  1. Fixed costs
  2. Variable costs
- Improve sales mix

...improve gearing through productivity gains – not just brutal cost-cutting!...

Purpose

The Strategic Growth Focus Model (SGFM) is a high-level framework which highlights the two dominant paths to sales/margin growth that can be *simultaneously* adopted by AMs. By increasing *volume* and improving *efficiency*, AMs can drive sustainable growth. The SGFM is useful because 'pulling the price lever' as a means to increase sales is often unavailable to AMs (and is proven to have little long-term impact on sustainable growth); whereas the options highlighted by the model (which is an extension of Ansoff's Paths to Growth Model with efficiency/cost and margin dimensions) are largely within the AMs orbit of control.

Components and Principles

The SGFM focuses upon the two main strategic paths to increase long-term organic growth, namely, increasing volume and improving efficiency:

1. *Increase Volume (Sales)*
   a) *Expand Market* – through converting/attracting new users (advocacy and marketing) and entering new segments
   b) *Market Penetration* – through increasing usage rates (visit frequency) and/or customer SPH, 'stealing' competitor customers and launching new products/services

2. *Improve Efficiency (Costs/Margins)*

    a) *Reduce Costs* – through bringing down fixed costs (rents, rates etc.) and reducing variable costs (labour, energy, COGs, OMCs etc.)

    b) *Increasing Prices* – usually outside the AM's span of control and inadvisable for most products unless it is accompanied by effective 'value engineering' (such as cheaper sourcing, a reduction in central overheads, compensating margin recovery from other goods/sales etc.)

    c) *Improving Sales Mix* – upselling higher margin items to increase net profit.

Issues

- **Efficiency Emphasis** – inevitably, most MUEs will expect AMs to drive the efficiency element of the model; particularly focussing upon the reduction of variable costs (labour, wastage etc.). However, it is crucial that AMs improve the gearing of their P&Ls not through slash and burn but through simultaneously preventing overhead creep whilst driving the sales line to increase margin and profit. In reality, in tight businesses, sustainable efficiencies and increased productivity will not be achieved on the variable cost line without commensurate investment in machinery, technology and people capability.

- **Applying the Price Lever** – in spite of the options offered up by this model, organisations will often resort to tactical price decreases or 'bundled offers' (through digital vouchering, BOGOFs, WIGIG, promotional drives etc.) to stimulate traffic. These are fine if they are used sparingly as rewards for existing customers and incentives to attract non/lapsed users. However, if these price cuts are incorporated permanently into the business model, significant re-engineering will be required to accommodate this new margin structure, higher volumes will have to (permanently) compensate for price reductions and/or suppliers will have to agree to reduce their wholesale pricing.

How AMs can use this Model

AMs should examine the gearing of their business (costs in relation to sales) and seek ways in which, without giving away margin, they can drive *volumes* whilst simultaneously increasing *efficiency*.

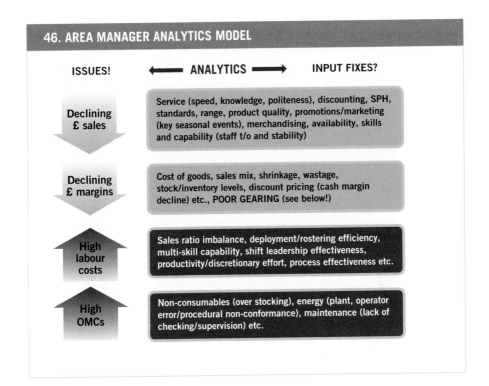

46. AREA MANAGER ANALYTICS MODEL

ISSUES!	← ANALYTICS →	INPUT FIXES?

Declining £ sales → Service (speed, knowledge, politeness), discounting, SPH, standards, range, product quality, promotions/marketing (key seasonal events), merchandising, availability, skills and capability (staff t/o and stability)

Declining £ margins → Cost of goods, sales mix, shrinkage, wastage, stock/inventory levels, discount pricing (cash margin decline) etc., POOR GEARING (see below!)

High labour costs → Sales ratio imbalance, deployment/rostering efficiency, multi-skill capability, shift leadership effectiveness, productivity/discretionary effort, process effectiveness etc.

High OMCs → Non-consumables (over stocking), energy (plant, operator error/procedural non-conformance), maintenance (lack of checking/supervision) etc.

Purpose

The AM Analytics Model highlights some of the connections/linkages between P&L issues (declining sales, decreasing margins, high labour costs and escalating OMCs) and some of their potential contributory causes/fixes. AMs should look for patterns of dysfunctionality across their district and units, and make both qualitative and quantitative connections to come up with appropriate solutions to arrest and/or turnaround these challenges.

Components and Principles

This model is divided into four major issue categories which are linked with numerous input fix options (non-controllables such as fixed costs and depreciation are excluded):

1. **Declining Sales** – attributable causal factors that AMs should look to solve include: poor levels of service (evidenced by company customer satisfaction surveys and spontaneous social-media site comments), deep discounting (without any volume recovery), falling item sales, declining spends per head (a migration to lower value items or smaller 'basket sizes'), poor standards (as shown up by audit scores), lack of promotion/ marketing 'cut through' during key events (seasonal and calendar), poor merchandising (lack of impulse spend), poor availability (evidenced by

exception report 'stock outs' and poor item sales), skills/capability issues (highlighted by poor stability, high turnover and low training completion) etc.

2. ***Declining Margins*** – AMs should examine the following potential contributing factors: high cost of goods (input inflation), sales mix imbalance (drift to lower margin items), shrinkage (theft), wastage (spoilt/returned goods and compensation payments), high stock/ inventory levels (causing items to be sold through at a discount), low pricing (resulting in poor cash margins), poor gearing (costs relative to sales – see below).

3. ***High Labour Costs*** – main reasons possibly being: sales ration imbalance (declining sales with unadjusted labour costs), over manning caused by deployment/rostering inefficiencies, lack of multi-skill capability (particularly during non-peak), poor productivity/discretionary effort (leading to role duplication and overmanning), lack of process efficiency (leading to costly human 'reworks' and recovery) etc.

4. ***High Other Management Costs (OMCs)*** – overstocking of non-consumables (cleaning materials etc.), inefficient energy usage (plant or operator error), high maintenance charges (poor infrastructure and/or lack on on-site contractor supervision) etc.

Issues

- **Uncontrollables** – whilst many input fixes can be applied by AMs to resolve P&L issues, several stand outside their remit or sphere of influence. Product design/evolution, range, pricing, amenity investment, central promotions/marketing and the 'employment brand' are likely to be controlled centrally. The AM must therefore assess what tools/levers (s)he has at his/her disposal and act swiftly to influence sales/margin/cost outcomes at a local level.
- **Causal Strength** – some issues will have several influencing causal factors – but which one is the most relevant 'input fix'? Inevitably the AM needs to experiment through trial and error, learning fast from the fruits of success or failure, to establish what commonly works and what doesn't.

How AMs can use this Model

This model can act as an analytical prompt for AMs to ask the following questions:
- What are the big P&L performance issues on my district or within specific units?
- Are there any major themes, patterns or trends?
- What are the appropriate fixes? Do these solutions fit with the problem – will their application drive positive outcomes?

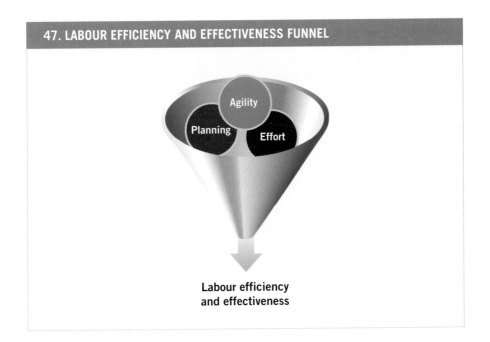

Labour efficiency
and effectiveness

Purpose

One major area in which AMs are constantly called upon to make adjustments/interventions – given the proportionately high cost to MUEs (Multi-Unit Enterprises) – is the labour line ratio (i.e. cost of labour as a percentage of sales). Fixing labour costs when they have run out of control is a major bugbear of AMs. How do MUEs and AMs set themselves up for success; controlling labour costs without blowing up the business? Many companies rely on central command and control mechanisms (predictive scheduling systems, labour 'controllers' who visit units and remodel rotas in keeping with sales patterns etc.). But ultimately labour management in businesses that are highly susceptible to violent 'peak and trough' swings (e.g. hospitality and leisure, due to calendar events and the weather) need to be flexible and responsive 'on the ground'. Indeed, labour scheduling and capacity management is both an art and a science, in which the AM and his/her GMs have a key role to play. The Labour Efficiency and Effectiveness Funnel highlights three key areas (agility, planning and effort) that all combine to improve labour P&L outcomes.

Principles and Components

1. *Agility* – the start point for ensuring responsiveness is ensuring that the key on-site decision makers are properly incentivised and equipped to scale labour up and down according to needs:
   a) *GM accountability* – i.e. link bonuses to t/o and labour spend (e.g.

wage bill multiplied by 4.5 to set the t/o target – t/o 'over target' results in 15% bonus split amongst colleagues)

  b) *On-site flexibility* – contracts (seasonal 'flex'), core/peripheral (full time vs part time), annualised hours, late-notice shift swap/reduction facilities.

2. **Planning** – accurate forecasting is also required, combined with effective capacity design and on-site experts who understand the local market:

  a) *Accurate demand forecasting* – last year/current year 'run rate'/ upcoming events/weather/monthly 'payday' calendar

  b) *Capacity design* – manning levels, key role 'fills' (shift leaders, hosts, production, service etc.), accounting for holidays/absence/maternity

  c) *Work/job design* – designated roles and responsibilities, multi-skilling

  d) *Process simplicity* – simplifying the service delivery system through removing unnecessary process stages (touch points) and/or solving pinchpoints through investment in technology, facilities and/or machivery enablers

  e) *Unit-level labour 'lead'* – responsibility designated to experienced personnel with micro-market knowledge.

3. **Effort** – ultimately discretionary effort (the ability to do more, better – with less!) will also contribute to labour efficiency and effectiveness:

  a) *Deployment* – rostering ('right complement, right people, right jobs, right time!'), linking staffing to volume and capacity, accounting

  b) *Store/shift leadership* – 'in session' motivation of high performers, REMOVAL OF POOR PERFORMERS

  c) *Extrinsic motivators* – rewards and incentives (session/day/week/ month/quarter/annual)

  d) *Intrinsic motivators* – attraction, development, avenues for progression, empowerment (complaint resolution), resources to do the job, honouring promised hours/holidays.

Issues

- **Kneejerk Cuts** – the issue that most AMs face at various junctures is a demand from the centre to cut labour 'immediately', either as result of poor trading or the need to 'hit the numbers' at key financial calendar points (quarterly, half year or full year). What does the AM do? Effective AMs will have built up sufficient emotional credit with their teams to respond; but this might be spent after wave upon wave of cuts and the imposition of cash targets. What good AMs do is anticipate when and where labour clampdowns are likely to be applied and have 'plans *A, B* and *C*' up their sleeves to ameliorate their worst excesses.

- **Service Impact** – the inevitable consequence of kneejerk cuts will be to endanger service provision, threatening the reputation of the business.

Again, AMs must ensure that they apply cuts that will have the least impact on customer perceptions of service. Untargeted, lazy, savage reductions will set their businesses back, degrading their sales/labour ratios even further, resulting in calls for further cuts! Good AMs will co-opt labour experts in their districts to 'do the right thing' regarding hours reductions rather than just 'doing it right' (i.e. just hitting the target).

How AMs can use this Framework

AMs can use this Labour Efficiency and Effectiveness Framework as a checklist to ask the following questions:

- **Agility** – are my units properly set up (in terms of GM incentives and contract flexibility) to respond to *violent* sales peaks and troughs?
- **Planning** – are my units rigorously forecasting demand and planning labour schedules accordingly? Are my units set up for maximum productivity; have we resolved pinchpoints caused by defective facilities, machinery or technology that are currently being overcompensated for by extra labour at present?
- **Effort** – are we deploying highly skilled and motivated 'A Teams' at peak to drive service and sales effectively?

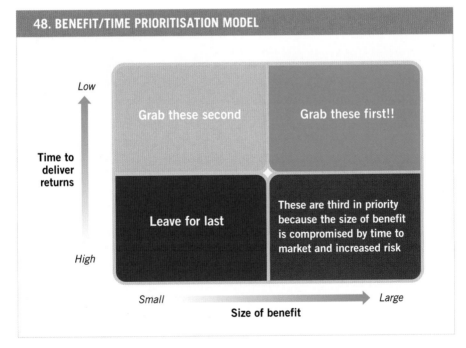

48. BENEFIT/TIME PRIORITISATION MODEL

- Time to deliver returns — Low / High
- Grab these second
- Grab these first!!
- Leave for last
- These are third in priority because the size of benefit is compromised by time to market and increased risk
- Size of benefit — Small / Large

Purpose

The Benefit/Time Prioritisation Model highlights where AMs should devote their efforts when prioritising key activities/initiatives within their districts.

Priority activity is determined by the amount of time to deliver a return set against the size of benefit. A benefit is defined not only as a major sales driver or margin gain but also defensive action to mitigate the costs of legal non-compliance.

Components and Principles

Activities should be prioritised in the following order:

1. *Large Benefit/Low Delivery Time* – here the AM can accelerate returns from 'big rock' opportunities; they involve large sales/margin upticks or major variable cost savings. These should be targeted first.
2. *Small Benefit/Low Delivery Time* – so called 'low hanging fruit' and 'quick wins', the AM can drive multiple small opportunities that add up to a 'big number' and give their teams a sense of momentum. These should be grabbed second because of their attractive benefit/time ratio.
3. *Large Benefit/High Delivery Time* – slow-burn tank busters which are hampered by time constraints – these need to be set in motion by the AM with the appropriate allocated resources. These are third in priority because of their delayed benefit (possibly in the next financial year).
4. *Small Benefit/High Delivery Time* – relatively non-value-added activities (such as attending dead man's committees and fulfilling time-wasting requests) which the AM should avoid.

Issues

- **Analysis** – AMs must have conducted a thorough analysis of the key opportunities in their district that will either increase volumes or improve efficiency (see previous model), placing them in rank order. Thorough analysis precedes prioritisation; however, AMs have a tendency – often due to the prospect/promise of overblown benefits with quick returns – to rush in.
- **Static/Dynamic** – this model suggests stasis; that is to say, activities can be ranked according to benefit/time metrics as part of a quarterly or half-yearly planning exercise. However, very often opportunities can switch categories and the AM needs to be agile, reprioritising on a constant basis to optimise benefit capture.

How AMs can use this Model

AMs should place their opportunities into one of the four categories in accordance with their scale of benefit juxtaposed against time to deliver in the current financial year (it helps if they have completed this process prior to the start). AMs should pursue categories 1 and 2 above with vigour, kick-off and monitor category 3 and dismiss category 4. They should also factor in the levels of resource and assistance required to realise key opportunities, rather than expecting them to be accomplished out of thin air.

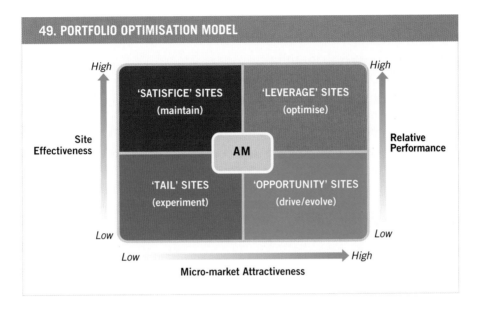

Purpose

The Portfolio Optimisation Model (POM) is a tool that the AM can use to discriminate between categories of sites in their district, based upon their analysis of site effectiveness, local market attractiveness and relative performance. No single unit in their portfolio is in exactly the same predicament: operational effectiveness will vary as will the competitive aspects local micro-markets. It is the role of AMs to analyse where their respective units lie in terms of relative performance, ensuring that they apply the right solutions (optimise, maintain, drive/evolve and experiment) to the right sites to optimise their portfolio.

Principles and Components

Relative unit performance will be contingent on two main factors:

1. *Site Effectiveness* – factors here within the control of the organisation will be influenced by both the centre and local operations. These include: brand positioning, site position, scale, layout, amenity, range, daypart coverage (mono or multi occasion), pricing, promotion (all largely dictated by the centre) and GM/team capability, store culture, productivity, quality, service execution, standards adherence, systems implementation, safety compliance and community connection (largely locally determined).

2. ***Micro-Market Attractiveness*** – factors here are outside of the firm and the AM's control but have huge impact on the performance of individual units. These include: competition, demographics, footfall/traffic, local labour market, 'officialdom', transport infrastructure, local supply chain and complementarity with other offers.

The above factors will determine whether or not units fall into one of four categories, requiring specific actions by AMs:

1. ***'Leverage'*** (High Site Effectiveness/High Micro-Market Attractiveness) – here AMs should *optimise* performance by maintaining their units' momentum by not taking their eyes off the ball. These sites will be high-yielding profit-centres and must be leveraged.

2. ***'Satisfice'*** (High Site Effectiveness/Low Micro-Market Attractiveness) – these sites should be *maintained* at their current performance levels, which are constrained by adverse local micro-market conditions. The GMs in these sites are doing the best job they possibly can: it is the AMs role to provide maximum support and recognition to ensure they are 'satisficed'.

3. ***'Opportunity'*** (Low Site Effectiveness/High Micro-Market Attractiveness) – AMs must concentrate their efforts upon *driving* performance in these underperforming assets (moving them up into the leverage category) by evolving/changing/improving aspects of their operations. The external micro-market is benign but these units fall short operationally. Improving incremental performance in these units is a major opportunity for the AM.

4. ***'Tail'*** (Low Site Effectiveness/Low Micro-Market Attractiveness) – some senior policy makers will have given up on these sites, possibly designating them 'non-core' and resigning them to a disposal list to be 'got rid of' at the earliest opportunity. Ambitious AMs will want to improve their relative performance and – given their lack of attention by the company – will probably have huge licence to *experiment* with their offer and operations.

Issues

- **Controllables** – the AM must discriminate between what (s)he can and cannot influence to drive performance within the context of the organisation/brand. Some AMs will have more latitude than others regarding aspects such as promotions, pricing and capital investment. One major controllable they do have is determining/shaping operational excellence at unit level through effective leadership and management practices.

- **Micro-Market Data** – organisations are not generally good at providing AMs with local market data (focussing instead on providing internal metrics/measures). It is beholden upon the AM and his/her team, therefore, to establish what the local micro-market climate of their units is. If it is hostile and threatening, how can they respond? If it is relatively benign, how can they 'fill their boots'?

How AMs can use this Model

Having rigorously analysed their portfolio, AMs should ask themselves the following questions:
- What performance categories do my sites fall into?
- What remedial actions do I need to take either:
  a) to sustain my leverage and satisfice sites' relative performance, or
  b) to improve my tail and opportunity sites' relative performance?

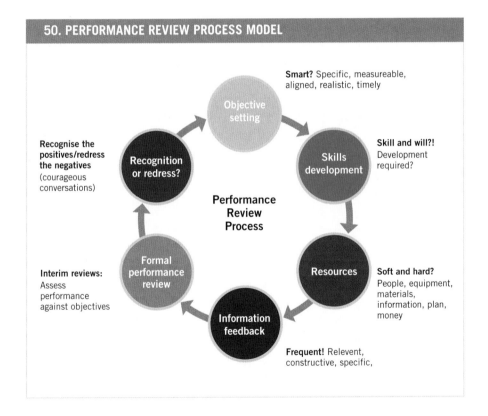

50. PERFORMANCE REVIEW PROCESS MODEL

Smart? Specific, measureable, aligned, realistic, timely

Objective setting

Skill and will?! Development required?

Skills development

Recognition or redress?

Recognise the positives/redress the negatives (courageous conversations)

Performance Review Process

Resources

Soft and hard? People, equipment, materials, information, plan, money

Formal performance review

Interim reviews: Assess performance against objectives

Information feedback

Frequent! Relevent, constructive, specific,

Purpose

The Performance Review Process Model (PRPM) illustrates the typical stages in a one-to-one boss–subordinate formal performance discussion.

These reviews are usually built into the organisational 'financial year' calendar of events (full and half year) although AMs can use the process at various junctures during the financial year to monitor/chase progress against KPIs and key objectives.

Components and Principles

The various sub-components of the process are:

1. ***Objective Setting*** – usually done at the beginning of the financial calendar with objectives being anchored/aligned to the P&L budget and cascaded scorecard KPIs. As incentives are attached to many of the targeted outcomes, it is crucial that the recipient views at least 50–70% of the goals at attainable.

2. ***Skills Development*** – if extra skills and knowledge are required for target fulfilment purposes, a personal development plan should accompany the PRP. However, AMs must check not only for skill but also the will to accomplish agreed goals.

3. ***Resources*** – in order to ensure buy-in, AMs must ensure (within reason) that appropriate enablers are in place to facilitate achievement of objectives – people, equipment and financial contingencies (for marketing/promotion etc.).

4. ***Informal Feedback*** – as the year progresses, AMs should informally chase progress, giving out appropriate signals on desired levels of performance.

5. ***Formal Performance Monitoring*** – at various times, the AM will convene meetings to monitor progress formally. Courageous conversations must ensue at this point: what should the GM stop, start or continue doing to reach his/her targets? What can the AM do to help? Remedial actions to bridge any gaps should be agreed and expedited immediately by both parties.

6. ***Recognition/Redress*** – during or at the end of the annual PRP process, due recognition should be made for progress (absolute or relative) through scoring, reward or notification. Poor performance will require immediate redress accompanied by a recovery plan. If the issue is capability, training and development will be the likely solution. If it is wilful behavioural non-conformance, other avenues of action might have to be pursued (formal action or a 'car-park chat').

Issues

- **Realism** – often, some KPIs and objectives (having been fashioned by senior policy makers detached from the reality of day-to-day operations) will be aspirational rather than realisable. The AM must therefore manage the subordinate's motivational levels throughout the process, placing an emphasis on recognising *relative* rather than *absolute* performance.

- **Timeliness** – at times, objectives are cascaded down the chain from the centre well into the financial year. Effective AMs will pre-empt this by planning growth initiatives/drives well in advance with their GMs and teams so that they are set up for success on day one.
- **Bounded Behaviours** – if budgets or KPIs are completely unrealistic or too soft (easy to beat), GMs and their teams might shirk – keeping back things for next year!

How AMs can use this Model

AMs must use this process to have open and uninhibited discussions with their subordinates. Indeed, they should use some of the tools in this book to analyse where their businesses are and how they can take them to the next level. AMs should inject energy and grounded enthusiasm into their discussions with PRP recipients, generating positive 'can dos' rather than accepting disillusioned 'can't/won't dos'!

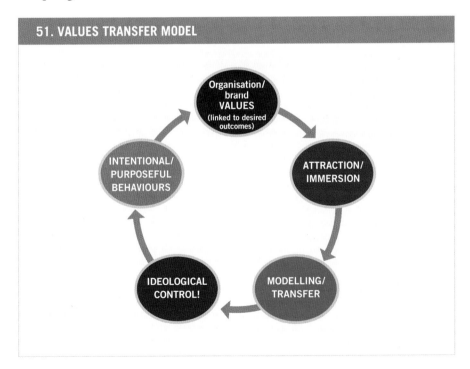

51. VALUES TRANSFER MODEL

Purpose

Most organisations have a set of espoused values (such as Burberry's 'Protect, Explore, Inspire') which attempt to codify required behaviours ('the way in which we do things around here'). These are intended to shape attitudes and guide purposeful/intentional behaviours that provide moral standards for ethical conduct within the organisational 'clan'. The Values Transfer Model (VTM) demonstrates how values transference typically operates in MUEs where values systems are particularly important given the dispersal of sites and their physical distance from the centre.

Components and Principles

Values systems are a 'soft' type of ideological control system (as opposed to previous models based around 'hard' bureaucratic controls) which assist the execution of an organisation's processes/practices in the right way. To this extent (unlike checking, monitoring, correction and coercion) values are an extremely effective – and cheap! – method of stimulating assured outcomes; *if* they are inculcated and disseminated in the right manner.

1. *Organisational/Brand Values* – successful ones are clear, simple, well-articulated and resonate with what the organisation is trying to achieve and what it stands for. (They are often referred to as 'organisational DNA', being derived from the company's 'brand archaeology'!)
2. *Hiring/Immersion* – successful systems filter hires according to 'values fit' and have immersion (induction) programmes that reinforce the 'way we act and do things around here'.
3. *Modelling/Transfer* – leaders within the organisation constantly reinforce the values through their communications and *consistent* decision making.
4. *Ideological Control* – organisations are now able to exert some positive ideological control over how people *think* and rather than just threatening bureaucratic monitoring control.
5. *Intentional/Purposeful Behaviours* – this ideological control results in intentional and purposeful behaviours by clan members that provide outcome surety for the organisational leadership (especially with regards to legal compliance and safety).

Issues

- **Cultural** – in international organisations, subsidiaries or partners might – due to different base value contexts – be misaligned to company values. (For example, the degree to which US libertarian values translate into high-context, collectivist cultures with a history of central coercion is questionable.)
- **Mixed Messages** – in spite of phrases such as 'we all live the values', some senior leadership cadres will act in contrarian/hypocritical ways, sending out mixed messages to their subordinates.

- **Prior Socialisation** – in spite of the best efforts of organisations, some people – due to prior birth, imprint and socialisation phases – will not have the capacity or will to change their values set. (This is particularly evident with the emerging millennial supply of labour in developed economy contexts, members of which – due to a life in cyberspace – often have poor social and communications skills.)

How AMs can use this Model

AMs should use this model to ask themselves the following questions:
- Do I live the company values (in terms of behaviour, demeanour and consistent decision making)?
- Do my followers understand what the company values are? Have we incorporated them into the way in which we do things in my district?
- Are there extra values that we – as a team – can add to improve *self-regulating* behaviours (i.e. togetherness, leaving egos outside the door, hardworking etc.)?
- If some of my followers fall outside of our prescribed/agreed value set, do they 'feel the electricity' of the district and/or organisation?

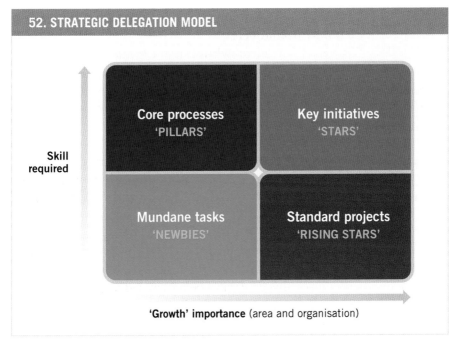

Purpose

The art of delegation is a major survival technique for overloaded AMs, increasing their installed capacity to work and perform by 'spreading the load'. The Strategic Delegation Model (SDM) illustrates (with the assistance of the previous Performance/Potential Matrix Model) how AMs should delegate activities/core process expertise within their districts. According to the level of skill required and their growth importance to the district, activities (change initiatives, standard projects and mundane tasks) and core process responsibilities/expertise (labour scheduling, service execution, promotions, compliance, talent management etc.) should be delegated out to stars, pillars, rising stars and newbies according to capability.

Components and Principles

Delegation can be assigned in many forms – formal, pragmatic, strategic, incremental, ad hoc, opportunistic and cultural. Strategic delegation is the best option for AMs – in this paradigm specific skills/capabilities are *purposefully* fitted with business needs. The typologies of strategic delegation in the SDM are as follows:

1. ***Key Initiatives*** – here high-value-added initiatives with high growth importance are delegated to 'stars' with high levels of technical, behavioural and cognitive skills.
2. ***Core Processes*** – core processes have a 'medium' growth impact given their basic, transactional nature but require a high degree of technical skill – hence their delegation to 'pillars' who have low levels of long-term potential but are crucial in keeping the day-to-day wheels of the district turning!
3. ***Standard Projects*** – projects that are important to the organisation but require low levels of technical skill (principal skills thinking and tenacity) can be assigned to 'rising stars' who can demonstrate their potential to migrate to key initiatives in the future.
4. ***Mundane Tasks*** – routine tasks that require expediting on the district should be assigned to 'newbies' in order to test their levels of energy and commitment whilst they learn the ropes.

Issues

- **Incorrect Designation** – AMs always run the risk of incorrectly matching skills with assigned responsibilities. More pertinently, however, AMs must establish that nominated personnel not only have the skill but also the will and incentive to expedite their responsibilities professionally.
- **Responsibility not Accountability** – although specific individuals within the district will have responsibility for the various assigned categories, overall accountability will still reside with the AM (especially for centrally led initiatives) and individual GMs (in terms of core process execution within their units).

How AMs can use this Model

AMs should ask themselves whether or not they are practising strategic delegation; that is to say, matching appropriate skills and capabilities against important growth activities and core process execution rather than delegating in a scattergun, ad hoc, opportunistic manner. Useful questions they can ask themselves include:

- Have I got my highest-potential people driving the most important growth initiatives?
- Have I got all the important core processes covered by technical experts (core process leaders, scorecard champions, houses of excellence etc.)?

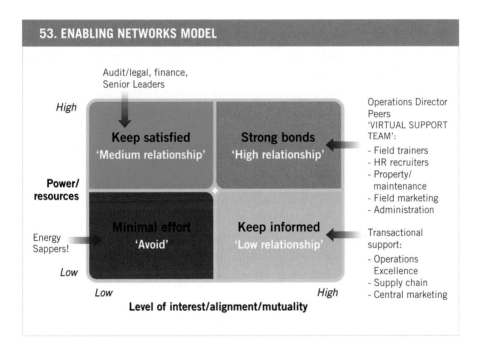

53. ENABLING NETWORKS MODEL

Audit/legal, finance, Senior Leaders

High

Keep satisfied
'Medium relationship'

Strong bonds
'High relationship'

Operations Director Peers
'VIRTUAL SUPPORT TEAM':
- Field trainers
- HR recruiters
- Property/ maintenance
- Field marketing
- Administration

Power/ resources

Energy Sappers!

Minimal effort
'Avoid'

Keep informed
'Low relationship'

Transactional support:
- Operations Excellence
- Supply chain
- Central marketing

Low

Low — High

Level of interest/alignment/mutuality

Purpose

The Enabling Networks Model (ENM) highlights the level and depth of relationships that AMs should foster with key stakeholders within their organisations based on their level of power and/or access to resources and congruence with the AM's role and objectives. In MUEs there are a number of actors who can help the AM and his/her district teams expedite their jobs more effectively – it is the role of the AM to leverage a 'virtual team' and coalition of enabling forces to help them achieve their performance objectives.

Components and Principles

The AM's direct line reports are likely to be operational meaning that (s)he has to tap into other parties within the organisation (along with other 'competing' AMs) to get the job done. The issue is how the AM prioritises and targets these enabling networks through the level/type of relationship (s)he fosters with certain key personnel:

1. ***Strong Bonds (high relationship)*** – the AM must create strong bonds with organisational players that have a high degree of direct power (such as their boss) and extensive resource access (such as their AM Peers and virtual team from support functions; HR business partners, recruitment and training officers, marketing assistants, property/maintenance managers, administration officers etc.) who are intrinsically aligned – for the purposes of their own KPI fulfilment – to the success of the district. These personnel help drive important inputs on the scorecard so are high value added to the AM and his/her team.

2. ***Keep Satisfied (medium relationship)*** – this cohort has a high power/resource index but – for practical and operational reasons – possesses a middling degree of mutuality with the AM and his/her team (being more detached from the day-to-day operations of the district). This cohort – which largely monitors outputs from the district – includes audit/legal, finance and senior leaders.

3. ***Keep Informed (low relationship)*** – this group has a high level of alignment/interest in what the AM and his team are doing but a low level of power resource to affect outcomes. Personnel fitting into this category might include: supply chain (purchasing), central marketing and operational excellence (productivity specialists).

4. ***Minimal Effort (no relationship)*** – this cohort has low levels of power resource and low levels of alignment with the AM and his/her team. AMs should avoid anybody in this category that would include energy sappers and self-interested opportunists who will fail to reciprocate or add value.

Issues

- **Behaviour to Outsiders** – often AMs will create a siege mentality in their districts by encouraging disdain for 'outsiders' because they 'haven't done the hard yards in operations' and/or 'they don't understand what we do'. This behaviour is exceptionally immature and potentially self-harming. Effective AMs are inclusive rather than exclusive – but they concentrate their relational efforts on the organisational players who have a high degree of mutual interest and will truly add 'something to the party'.

- **Creating Strong Bonds** – AMs have to create a 'virtual team' outside of their immediate direct reports; the problem is that they will invariably be competing against other interests for their time and resources. The question is how the AM 'makes his/her agenda their agenda.' This can be achieved by understanding how they can contribute to the goals of potential allies, showing empathy for the challenges/problems their friends face (understanding their world), uncovering hidden value for helpers and regularly praising/recognising their contribution.

How AMs can use this Model
AMs should consider with *whom* in the organisation and *how* they create really strong bonds, in order to build a high-performing 'virtual team' that will help them to drive district growth!

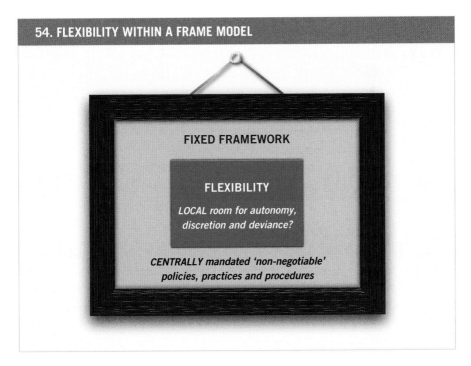

54. FLEXIBILITY WITHIN A FRAME MODEL

FIXED FRAMEWORK

FLEXIBILITY

LOCAL room for autonomy, discretion and deviance?

CENTRALLY mandated 'non-negotiable' policies, practices and procedures

Purpose
The Flexibility within a Frame Model (FFM) illustrates that whilst organisations centrally mandate various fixed policies, procedures and practices, they generally allow some flexibility for local autonomous behaviour. They do this for two reasons: first, to build a degree of local responsiveness and agility into their business model at micro-market level and, second, to enrich frontline operators' job roles through providing a certain degree of autonomy and self-expression. Paradoxically, organisations that allow a degree of local autonomy actually find that they are able to extract better 'core' control of their operations in exchange. The degree to

which operators will be granted 'flexibility within a frame' will be dependent on two principal factors: the culture of the organisation (a belief in 'tight' compliance or 'loose' empowerment) and/or the degree of 'hard' tightly prescribed or 'soft' customised branding.

Components and Principles

1. *Fixed Framework* – these are centrally mandated policies usually incorporating the brand blueprint and standard operating procedures (BOH and FOH). These elements underpin the efficiency of the organisation – ensuring consistency and dependability of execution – and are regularly monitored/audited to ensure conformance and compliance.

2. *Flexible Framework* – outside these prescribed ways of working, the AM and his/her team might have a certain amount of latitude with regards to addressing the local market (e.g. range, local promotions and social media 'marketing' etc.).

Issues

- **Pendulum Effect** – often organisations will swing from *tight* to *loose* and back to *tight* again. Why? Companies are likely to *tighten* up procedures during challenging commercial conditions (as a form of control comfort blanket) or during regime change (to ensure outcome certainty during honeymoon performance periods), gradually *loosening* grip over time as confidence improves – only to revert back to *tight* if they perceive they are losing control. These pendulum swings are confusing and derailing for frontline operators who fear coercion and punishment if levels of compliance tighten and are suspicious/mistrusting when a looser approach is granted.

- **Deviance** – in some instances, AMs and their GMs will ignore the rules and laws of the organisation to operate semi-autonomously in a deviant manner in order to generate growth. This so-called 'added-value deviance' is dangerous when exercised by inexperienced or over-excited operators. Experienced operators will seek the explicit or tacit approval of higher authorities before they step outside the fixed framework in order to pursue a locally led growth agenda.

How AMs can use this Model

AMs should establish what the centrally mandated aspects of their operations are (especially those with a legal/regulatory dimension) and where their room for local autonomy lies. They should ask themselves: how far can I push the envelope in adapting the offer to the local market without 'blowing up' or compromising the brand?

SECTION 4

EVOLVE
Operations and Offer

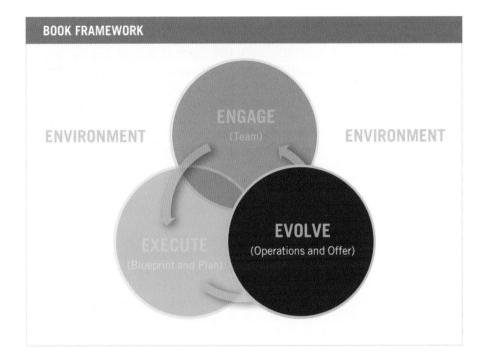

BOOK FRAMEWORK

ENVIRONMENT

ENGAGE
(Team)

ENVIRONMENT

EXECUTE
(Blueprint and Plan)

EVOLVE
(Operations and Offer)

Once the fundamental hygiene factor of execution has been achieved (aided by engagement), Area Managers can facilitate the organisation's change agenda and/or their own local adaptations to operations and the offer. These models provide insights and instruction into how successful Area Managers can facilitate top-down change and local evolution within the context of their district portfolio of idiosyncratic sites and micro-markets.

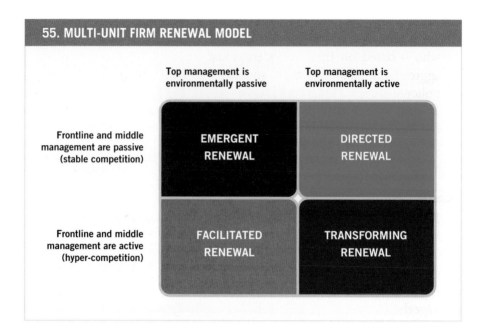

55. MULTI-UNIT FIRM RENEWAL MODEL

	Top management is environmentally passive	Top management is environmentally active
Frontline and middle management are passive (stable competition)	EMERGENT RENEWAL	DIRECTED RENEWAL
Frontline and middle management are active (hyper-competition)	FACILITATED RENEWAL	TRANSFORMING RENEWAL

Purpose

This Renewal Model, derived from one of the most widely cited academic articles[29] on MUEs, classifies the way in which multi-unit firms renew themselves from the extremes of a top-middle-down basis or a down-middle-up basis. Whether renewal is emergent, directed, facilitated or transforming is contingent upon the level of proactivity/activism or reactiveness/passiveness on the part of either the strategic leadership or the operational management within the MUE. It is a useful model because it conceptualises renewal as being the dynamic outcome of both levels of the leader/manager hierarchy within MUEs.

Components and Principles

The four main types of idealised renewal for multi-unit firms are as follows:

1. *Emergent Renewal* – here, both top and frontline/middle management are operating in stable markets with a passive environment; their bias to action in this situation is towards exploitation and following the market.

2. *Directed Renewal* – in this instance, an environmentally active top management is juxtaposed against a passive frontline/middle management in the face of seemingly stable competitive conditions; bias to action in this instance is exploration by top management.

---

29 Adapted from Volberda, H., Baden-Fuller, C., and van der Bosch, F. (2001) 'Mastering Strategic Renewal: Mobilising Renewal Journeys in Multi-Unit Firms', *Long Range Planning*, 34, pp.159–78.

3. *Facilitated Renewal* – in this category, MUEs have top managers who are environmentally passive confronted by frontline/middle management who – based on their knowledge/fear of local hyper competition – aggressively challenge their superiors in order to *ignite* changes in policy/direction.

4. *Transformational Renewal* – here, both cohorts are alive to the need for major renewal. Top management is environmentally active and frontline/middle management is active due to competitive threats. This shared sense-making leads to a *collaborative* bias for action.

Issues

- **Behaviour** – this model takes an idealised, one-size-fits-all view of behaviour within both managerial cohorts. The reality is that different divisions and brands within MUEs will adopt different approaches dependent on the disposition and quality of their top and frontline/middle management.

- **Overly Rational** – again, the model suggests that managers will rationally respond in certain ways given external circumstances. The reality is that managers embark on renewal journeys for a plethora of emotional reasons including ego, narcissism, hubris, exuberance and fear.

How AMs can use this Model

AMs should consider the type of renewal approach currently in train within their organisation. Is it appropriate? Are top management too passive in the face of emergent competition? If so, looking at the facilitated renewal option, is there anything you can do to ignite a competitive response (i.e. form coalitions of mutual interest to impact and influence top management thinking)?

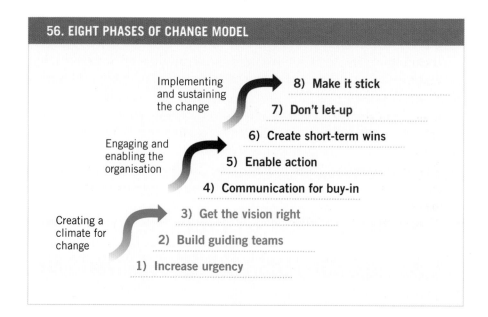

Implementing and sustaining the change

8) Make it stick

7) Don't let-up

6) Create short-term wins

Engaging and enabling the organisation

5) Enable action

4) Communication for buy-in

3) Get the vision right

Creating a climate for change

2) Build guiding teams

1) Increase urgency

Purpose

Kotter's famous model[30] conceptualises successful/sustainable change as transitioning through eight key phases. Based on his observations that change generally fails due to a number of common mistakes (complacency, no guiding coalition, lack of a clear vision, poor communication, allowing roadblocks to persist, no short-term momentum, declaring victory too soon and a failure to anchor change within the corporate culture), Kotter devised a model – which has since been viewed as the standard model of top-down change – as an effective antidote and managerial route map.

Components and Principles

The eight phases (which transition through a process of 'creating a climate for change', 'engaging and enabling the organisation' and 'implementing and sustaining the change') incorporate the following actions:

1. *Increase Urgency* – in order to overcome complacency, misplaced feelings of security must be eliminated through the creation of a 'burning platform' (i.e. technological disruption or 'barbarians at the gates').
2. *Build a Guiding Team* – a team with a shared purpose and understanding of the scale of the task accompanied with a belief in a successful outcome should be brought together. This strong coalition should be furnished with the necessary skills, reputation and network to lead the change agenda.

---

30 Adapted from Kotter, J.P. (1996) *Leading Change*, Harvard Business Review Press.

3. ***Get the Vision Right*** – the team must build a vision that bridges the current and future state. The vision ('where we want to get to') must be meaningful and compelling, and underpinned by sound strategy and tactics.
4. ***Communication for Buy-in*** – consistent and coherent messaging concerning the change which addresses the 'what's in it for me?' question for employees must be effectively disseminated across the whole organisation.
5. ***Enable Action*** – systems, processes and resources should be put in place to facilitate effective action, augmented by top team support for 'permission to succeed!'
6. ***Create Short-term Wins*** – because the change process might be lengthy and painful, 'recipients' should be encouraged to see that the plan has positive momentum and the final destination will be worthwhile by the visibility of a number of short-term wins.
7. ***Don't Let Up*** – gains should be consolidated but a relentless pace should continue in order to generate further gains.
8. ***Make it Stick*** – with major changes having been made, they must be made permanent by being embedded within the corporate culture ('the way in which we do things around here').

Issues

- **Big Bang** – change is not a one-off event: it should be part and parcel of an organisation's everyday life, particularly in current times given the potential threats/opportunities posed by the digital revolution.
- **Top-Down** – Kotter's model has a deterministic top-down feel which neglects down-middle-up dimensions to change.
- **Employees as Recipients** – employees are envisioned as being on the receiving end of change with little power/influence over its direction. This is a state that can encourage disillusionment and stress.

How AMs can use this Model

This model is an extremely useful tool for AMs who are planning wholesale changes for their district. It can be used as a route map to facilitate the change process, challenging/overcoming fundamental roadblocks that might resist fundamental change.

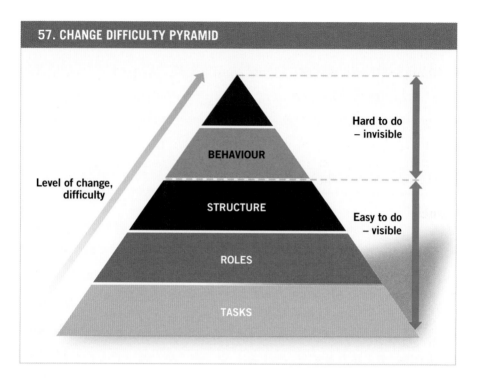

57. CHANGE DIFFICULTY PYRAMID

Hard to do
– invisible

BEHAVIOUR

Level of change,
difficulty

STRUCTURE

Easy to do
– visible

ROLES

TASKS

Purpose

The Change Difficulty Pyramid (CDP) illustrates the types of change that organisations invoke in response to, or in anticipation of, disruptive external forces (e.g. technological, customer and/or competitor) and their commensurate levels of difficulty. It assists managerial understanding of the differences between visible changes (tasks, roles and structure) which are relatively easy to enact and invisible changes (behaviours and culture) which are hard to implement/track.

Components and Principles

The Change Difficulty Pyramid is sub-divided into five categories which are, in turn, divided into two segments, according to levels of difficulty:

1. *Visible 'Easy to Do' Changes* – typically management will focus upon 'hard', tangible changes, possibly believing that they are the most costly/time-consuming part of the change process. This model makes it clear that this is a misconception: a formal process (in line with legal requirements) is followed, backed up by significant communication/ consultation that can (in relative terms) quickly transform the tasks, roles and structure of an organisation. Layoffs and new hires can seem to be expensive during the re-modelling process but they are the first and easiest step in making the organisation fit for purpose.

2. *Invisible 'Hard to Do' Changes* – these changes include altering behaviours and the prevailing culture, which is an exceptionally hard thing to achieve. Behaviours and culture are intangible and invisible but have a profound effect on the organisation's capability to execute a new strategy. Metaphorically speaking, if an organisation changes tasks, roles and structure without addressing mindsets and behaviours, it is merely 'shuffling deckchairs on the Titanic'. Significant investment in cultural reprogramming and (in some cases) new leadership are required to shift the soft DNA of the organisation.

Issues

- **Locating Resistance** – the problem with shifting behaviours lies in locating the type and nature of resistance (see the Categories of Resistance Model). Covert resistance can persist well into the change process and beyond because saboteurs keep their attitudes/prejudices well hidden.
- **Senior Behaviours** – sometimes senior policy makers will rely on others to get excited on their behalf about the changes, without necessarily getting engaged in it themselves; just focussing upon the outputs (cost savings, greater efficiencies etc.). Their idleness and inability to sell the benefits of change can have a devastating effect on current and future change programmes.

How AMs can use this Model

AMs should use this model to differentiate between easy-to-do, tangible task/role/structural change and hard-to-do, intangible behavioural/cultural change. They should consider what interventions they need to make to shift attitudes and behaviours in order to effect long-lasting and meaningful change (such as key changes in people, personal modelling and 'reorientation').

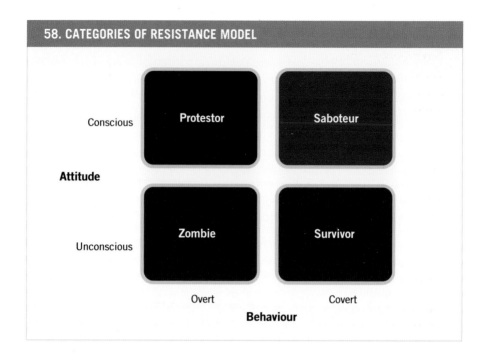

58. CATEGORIES OF RESISTANCE MODEL

Purpose

The Categories of Resistance Model (CRM) illustrates four archetypal categories of resistance behaviour (protestor, saboteur, survivor and zombie) during change/evolution processes which are manifested through conscious/unconscious attitudes and over/covert behaviours. This is a useful model for managers as it surfaces unconscious, hidden dimensions of 'resistor' behaviour.

Components and Principles

There are four variants of resistor behaviour:

1. **Protestor** – easily spotted by change managers, protestors openly declare their opposition to change. Once identified, their objections can be tackled and potentially ameliorated.

2. **Saboteur** – this category of resistor is consciously unhappy with the new proposed ways believing that the past 'was a better place'. However, saboteurs actions to subvert/undermine change processes are covert and hidden. They are difficult to identify but – because of their wilfulness – are the most dangerous category of resistor!

3. **Zombie** – these resistors have no real opinions of their own but are subconsciously influenced by protestors into opposing change. Easily led by dominant personalities/groups in the hierarchy, zombies

unconsciously resist but, if turned around by change makers, can make a positive contribution in the longer run.

4. *Survivors* – this group hangs around in the organisation whatever changes are in train, maintaining a self-interested survival strategy of malevolent silence. Hard to spot, they are 'reprogrammable' once identified.

Issues

- **Spotting the Coverts** – by definition, identifying covert resistors who hide their true feelings and agendas is highly difficult. It is useful for AMs to recognise that such categories exist and that they should be vigilant, watching for outcomes rather than attitudes, to identify passive resistors.

- **Static Attitudes/Behaviours** – this model presents a rather static representation of resistance when, in actual fact, feelings and actions amongst followers will fluctuate according to situation. Followers might adopt a resistant mindset to cost-cutting measures, for example, whilst simultaneously adopting a proactive disposition towards sales growth initiatives.

How AMs can use this Model

AMs should consider who the overt/covert resistors within their district are and identify which categories they fall into. Dealing with the protestors first (because they are easily identifiable), AMs should attempt to turn and co-opt them in order to build a coalition which runs with proposed changes. Zombies and survivors should – once identified – be challenged to alter their mindsets. Saboteurs who refuse to change their conscious attitudes and continue with subversive behaviour should be removed from the field of play.

59. FORCE-FIELD ANALYSIS OF CHANGE MODEL

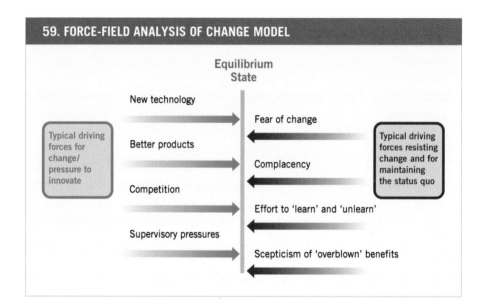

Purpose

The Force-Field Analysis of Change Model (FFACM) is a tool that can be used by managers to locate the typical forces that both drive *and* inhibit change. Building upon Lewin's force field theory of change[31] of 60 years ago, it proposes that managers should be able to maintain equilibrium (the business's centre of gravity) if they *simultaneously* deal with the countervailing forces of the change process.

Components and Principles

This model envisages organisations maintaining equilibrium (desired 'steady state') by reconciling 'drivers' and 'resistors' to change:

1. *Forces Driving Change* – in MUEs these are typically new technology ('push' and 'pull' mechanisms), better products (superior raw materials, packaging and configuration), competitive pressures (faster, smarter, better!) and supervisory pressures (requirement for growth).

2. *Forces Resisting Change* – countervailing forces include fear (disruption to status, security and identity), complacency (misguided arrogance), laziness (the effort to learn new ways and unlearn new habits) and scepticism of overblown benefits (recipients of change are wary of change makers who constantly 'polish the turd' by making overblown benefit statements). The Eight Phases of Change Model (see Model 58) provides some guidance as to how change makers can address some of these forces.

---

31 Lewin, K. (1951) *Field Theory in Social Sciences*, NY: Harper and Row.

Issues

- **Concept of Equilibrium** – this model conceives of organisations as maintaining a status quo in spite of the opposing forces of change. In reality, given the dynamic pace of change wrought through the digital revolution, it is doubtful whether any state of equilibrium can be sustained for long.

- **Identifying Forces** – this model rationally sees managers as having the capacity to identify dominant resistant forces. As the previous model (the Categories of Resistance Model) demonstrated, some attitudinal/behavioural forces are covert and hidden. Locating resistance is difficult when it has gone underground!

How AMs can use this Model

AMs should consider the forces driving change in their district and maturely devise a plan as to how they can offset/ameliorate their countervailing forces in order to maintain equilibrium.

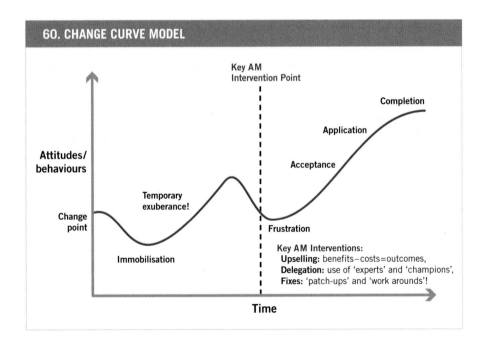

60. CHANGE CURVE MODEL

Purpose

Based on Kubler-Ross's loss transition curve, the Change Curve Model (CCM) illustrates the attitudinal/behavioural changes that individuals will generally go through during a major change process. It demonstrates how

AMs can intervene at a key point (generally the frustration stage) to help individuals transition to acceptance and beyond.

Components and Principles

Following the change point, recipients will generally experience the following feelings and emotions:

1. *Immobilisation* – those affected by change withdraw as they seek time to adjust to a new paradigm/situation.
2. *Denial* – after a brief 'up curve' of feelings of release, thoughts of denial set in as individuals begin to understand the scale of the task.
3. *Frustration* – realising that change isn't going to go away, they become frustrated because they feel ill equipped to make the changes in behaviour that are required.
4. *KEY INTERVENTION POINT* – at this stage of heightened frustration AMs can intervene by:
   - Upselling – outlining how benefits of the change will outweigh the personal costs by delivering positive outcomes (benefits – costs = outcomes)
   - Delegation – deploying 'expert' process champions to ease the change transition
   - Fixes – sanctioning 'patch-ups' and 'workarounds' to make changes fit for local purpose.
5. *Acceptance* – at this point, recipients accept necessary changes (possibly slightly adapted) and engage in the process of learning/absorbing new skills and knowledge.
6. *Application* – individuals apply their new learning and take responsibility for driving through the change.
7. *Completion* – change is embedded within the organisation.

Issues

- **Determinism** – the CCM implies that all individuals go through a sequential attitudinal/behavioural process of loss, adjustment, acceptance and moving on. The reality is that some individuals (due to personality, cognitive capability and aspiration) achieve acceptance without ever going through these phases.
- **Linear** – the change curve is linear in the sense that it conceives individuals transitioning from a negative to a positive mindset following the resolution of the frustration stage. In reality, individuals might transition to acceptance and then regress to frustration when they find that the promised tools/resources for change are defective or absent.

How AMs can use this Model

AMs have a pivotal role in MUEs in implementing major change initiatives but – in order to be effective – they must judge when they are really going to change gears and drive the change through. As the model shows, this is not necessarily at the change point because recipients need time to absorb what the change is and what personal sacrifices they must make. Ramping up their interventions at the frustration stage is an appropriate time to give the change some semblance of momentum.

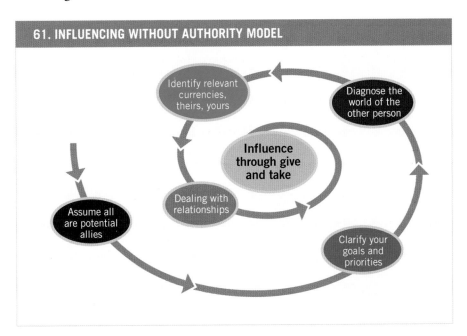

61. INFLUENCING WITHOUT AUTHORITY MODEL

Identify relevant currencies, theirs, yours

Diagnose the world of the other person

Influence through give and take

Dealing with relationships

Assume all are potential allies

Clarify your goals and priorities

Purpose

Within their districts, effective AMs will strategically delegate key processes and initiatives to nominated leads and champions (see Strategic Delegation Matrix). In addition, in some organisations, 'cluster' managers and leads (GMs who in addition to responsibility for their own unit have jurisdiction over a number of other units) are appointed, usually as span breakers between the AM and his/her units. The reality for all GMs appointed into, or nominated for, these roles is that their power is somewhat constrained due to a lack of positional/coercive power resource. Instead, they must exercise 'expert' power or 'relational influence' to fulfil their duties. This is something that is explored in more depth by the Influencing Without Authority (IWA) Model.[32]

32 Adapted from Cohen, A.R., and Bradford, D.L. (1989) *Influence without Authority*, NY: John Wiley.

Components and Principles

AMs can train their leads and champions to use the IWA by getting them to go through the following stages, and to ask themselves the associated questions:

1. *Assume all are Potential Allies* – instead of taking a confrontational ('why the hell can't you do it? – I can!') stance, ask yourself: what are our mutual interests? How can we get on?

2. *Clarify your Goals and Priorities* – look for commonalities, asking yourself: what common goals do we have? What are non-negotiables? What are their non-negotiables?

3. *Diagnose the World of the Other Person* – seeking first to understand, ask yourself: what pressures/forces are they subject to? How are they incentivised and/or coerced and punished? What false pre-conceptions do I have about their world – how do I put them to one side?

4. *Identify Relevant Currencies* (theirs and yours) – in light of the currencies you have that are of high exchange value (expertise, emotional support, information, influence with the AM etc.), ask yourself the following: what do they care about? How can I help them achieve what they want – making sure that they feel that they are getting something out of the relationship? What hidden value can I find for this person (i.e. something they get of high value that they didn't know existed)?

5. **Dealing with Relationships** – following engagement, ask yourself the following questions: how is the relationship evolving – is it positive, neutral or negative? If it is the latter, how do I make it more constructive?

6. *Influence through Give and Take* – as you start working together, ask yourself: are we reciprocating? Am I building indebtedness? Is this relationship now based on a long-term mutual trust?

Issues

• **Total Resistance** – the IWA Model is built around the presupposition that value-added relationships can be built through exercising referent power and high levels of targeted 'currency' exchange. In some instances, individuals will refuse to reciprocate (taking the currency but failing to deliver what has been agreed) because they are takers or just from sheer bloody-mindedness. Avoid/discard these people – concentrate your efforts on people that will become strong allies.

• **Time** – given the necessity for leads and champions to land/facilitate operational improvement and enhanced performance quickly, they might have insufficient time to go through the whole IWA process.

How AMs can use this Model

AMs should train their leads and champions in the art of IWA because attempts to influence peers into accepting/implementing change using empty threats will not work!

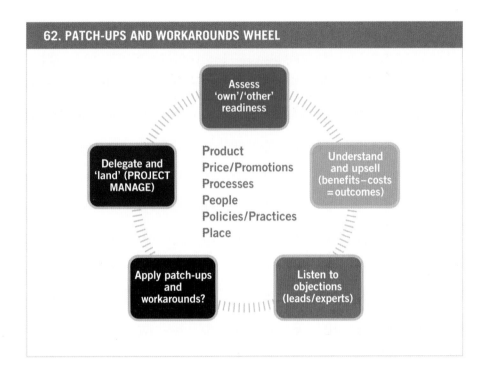

62. PATCH-UPS AND WORKAROUNDS WHEEL

- Assess 'own'/'other' readiness
- Understand and upsell (benefits – costs = outcomes)
- Listen to objections (leads/experts)
- Apply patch-ups and workarounds?
- Delegate and 'land' (PROJECT MANAGE)

Product
Price/Promotions
Processes
People
Policies/Practices
Place

Purpose

The Patch-ups and Workarounds Wheel is a process model that illustrates how AMs should apply local fixes to centrally conceived initiatives and changes. Often changes will be promulgated by the centre in a one-size-fits-all manner (for the purposes of *efficiency*) but the AM needs to assess whether the proposed changes and their timetabling will lead to greater *effectiveness*; and if not, either 'patch-up' (i.e. make the initiative more workable in a local context) or apply 'workarounds' (i.e. meet the policy-makers' ends but not through the means they originally intended!). For the purposes of this model, the types of changes are classified as any part of the ***marketing mix*** (product, price, promotions, processes, people, practices and place).

Components and Principles

The Patch-ups and Workaround Wheel proposes that AMs follow a sequential process in order to apply changes to the change!

1. **Readiness** – AMs should firstly assess their own state of change readiness and that of others (followers). Where does resistance to change lie?
2. **Understand and Upsell** – having understood the broad principles and some of the minutiae of the change, the AM should upsell its benefits at the appropriate time (benefits – costs = outcomes).
3. **Listen to Objections** – AMs should simultaneously listen to and take on board objections, co-opting process experts and leads within the district (with responsibility for various elements of the marketing mix) to make viable (and legal) proposals with regards to either the implementation timetable and/or the content of the proposed changes.
4. **Apply Patch-ups and Workarounds** – instigate and give permission for local alterations or solutions that help the organisation achieve its intended goals – although not through the originally intended means.
5. **Delegate** – grant responsibility to nominated personnel within the district (usually nominated process leads and champions) to project manage the 'adjusted' change.

Issues

- **Cheating** – if AMs give permission to their subordinates to patch-up or workaround with the express intention of cheating, gorging or skimming, they will be acting illegally (subverting the rules and values of the organisation). Sanctions may follow if they are caught out.
- **Inconsistency** – MUEs are designed around the principles of consistency, uniformity and dependability. Any patch-ups or workarounds that have a tangible impact on the consumer's perception of the brand (and could negatively affect the operations of other units) should be signed off by a higher authority.

How AMs can use this Model

AMs can use this model as a checklist in order to assess and verify the necessity for local adaptations. They must always be conscious, however, of the overarching imperative of considering/making added-value changes that add to rather than subtract from the sum of the MUE as a whole.

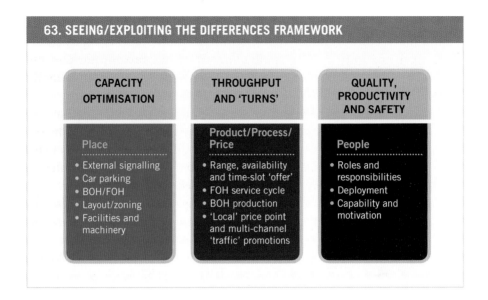

CAPACITY OPTIMISATION	THROUGHPUT AND 'TURNS'	QUALITY, PRODUCTIVITY AND SAFETY
Place	**Product/Process/Price**	**People**
• External signalling • Car parking • BOH/FOH • Layout/zoning • Facilities and machinery	• Range, availability and time-slot 'offer' • FOH service cycle • BOH production • 'Local' price point and multi-channel 'traffic' promotions	• Roles and responsibilities • Deployment • Capability and motivation

Purpose

This framework challenges AMs to see/exploit the differences/opportunities at a local level within their district. It highlights three output clusters (capacity optimisation; throughputs and 'turns'; quality/productivity and safety) that are attached to improvements that can be made to place, product/process/price and people. It further highlights the factors that AMs should dispassionately analyse to drive growth by leveraging/improving these areas (where this is permissible and affordable).

Components and Principles

This model is divided into three output/focus areas:

1. *Capacity Optimisation (Place)* – the AM's job is to sweat expensive land-based assets. Focusing upon place, they should check whether their units are properly 'signalled', have sufficient car parking (are staff using critical slots during trading?), BOH/FOH layout and 'traffic' flows are efficient and that there are sufficient facilities (e.g. toilets) and machinery (e.g. tills, handhelds and kitchen equipment in hospitality) to cope with demand.

2. *Throughputs and Turns* (Product, Process and Price) – AMs should ensure that throughputs (customer transactions/item sales) are optimised by examining factors such as: range, availability, daypart offer, FOH service-cycle efficiency, BOH production rhythms, local pricing fit, promotional offer timings, social-media PR etc.

3. *Quality, Productivity and Safety* (People) – in order to drive service/ product quality, productivity (output per staff member) and safety (particularly during peak trading times), AMs should examine the following areas with a view to making improvements: staff defined roles and responsibilities, micro-KPIs (session and shift), effective deployment and rostering (right person, right place, right time) and appropriate motivational/capability interventions (incentives, recognition, training and development etc.).

Issues

- **Cognitive Capacity** – the ability of AMs to work with teams/GMs to see the differences and exploit the opportunities is related to their levels of cognitive 'thinking' capability. Effective AMs will process what they see on a site-by-site basis and – making comparisons – will master the ability to locate the key variables that will drive performance forwards in any given unit. This is difficult for many AMs who have transitioned into the role from single-site roles because their worldview will be contaminated by what they did in their site rather than what will work in any given context.
- **Curiosity** – allied to this, AMs need to be curious about how they can do things faster, better and safer for their end customers. Successful AMs do not accept the status quo or leave opportunities unexploited/ unchallenged! Again, maintaining a sense of curiosity is difficult in hard branded environments where they have might have been conditioned to follow a strictly uniform approach.

How AMs can use this Model

AMs should – in unison with their GMs/teams – consider what LOCAL SOLUTIONS can be found/applied to drive growth within their district. They should question how they sweat their assets, driving throughputs and optimising productivity/quality by 'seeing the differences' and exploiting the opportunity to improve any element of the marketing mix (place, product, promotions, processes and people) that falls within their sphere of local influence.

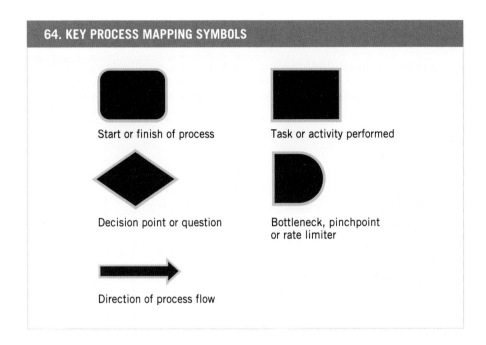

Start or finish of process

Task or activity performed

Decision point or question

Bottleneck, pinchpoint or rate limiter

Direction of process flow

Purpose

A process is the transportation of materials, customers or information through a sequence of *added-value* activity stages. Process Mapping is a means by which AMs can assess the efficiency and effectiveness of processes (i.e. service delivery, production and promotional mechanisms etc.) within their district. It helps them identify obsolete stages, bottlenecks or pinch points that inhibit the rhythm of the business, undermining fundamental process objectives of *least* cost (high sales), speed, dependability, safety, flexibility and quality. Easy to learn and teach, AMs can use this analytical tool to immeasurably improve their operations.

Components and Principles

Essentially, process mapping is a workflow instrument which, through diagrammatic representation, assists managerial insight into singular, multiple or parallel business processes. As part of the continuous process improvement function of AMs, it can be learnt through the understanding/ absorption of seven key steps:

1. ***Establish the parameters*** – where does the current 'as is' process start and end?
2. ***Document the Steps*** – first, use a verb to begin the task description and then, second, 'brain dump' the various stages in the current process.
3. ***Sequence the Steps*** – place the tasks and stages onto post-it notes so

that you can move them around – then place them in order of sequence.

4. ***Apply Symbols and Flow*** – apply the basic symbols (see above figure) around the sequential stages (encompassing activities and decision points):
   - Oval – represents the beginning (input) stage and end (output) stage
   - Rectangle– stands for the tasks or activities performed
   - Diamond – represents stages in the process where decisions are required or questions need addressing
   - Half Oval – stands for pinch points, blockages or 'rate limiters' which inhibit the rhythm of the process
   - Arrows – signify the direction of the process flow.

5. ***Check 'As Is' Map for Completeness*** – keep remodelling and working on the 'as is' process chart to ensure accuracy and completeness of current state. Then finalise.

6. ***Create 'To Be' Process Map*** – remove non-value-added activities and decision points that create bottlenecks in order to lower costs (increase sales) and increase speed, dependability, quality, safety etc. Remodel to create the 'ideal process'.

7. ***Transforming 'Enabling' Inputs*** – cost and plan the necessary transforming enabling inputs that will facilitate your 'To Be' state. These will usually include investment in staff (i.e. retraining), machinery (new or mended), technology and facilities (layout and flow). Ensure that you gain a positive ROI on this spend in the desired 'To Be' state.

Issues

- **Motives** – process mapping is a rational/scientific way to approach improving an operation. However, often the problem is not the process itself but the attitude and motivation of those engaged in executing it. Before you embark on improving a process, ask yourself whether it is the process that is defective or the people involved in delivering it!
- **Capturing the 'As Is' Process** – this can never be achieved at a distance – AMs need to co-opt experts or conduct intensive observation/investigation to cover all the stages.
- **Funding 'To Be'** – processes cannot be improved unless time and/or money is invested in staff, machinery, technology or facilities.

How AMs can use this Model

Continuous process improvement is a fundamental role performed by the AM. Learning and then applying the principles of process mapping will improve rhythm, throughputs and capacity/asset utilisation.

65. MULTI-UNIT KNOWLEDGE TRANSFER MODEL

Architecture
- **Geography:** clusters, families, 'hub and spoke', stores of excellence
- **Process:** leads, champions, experts

Formal Channels
District meetings, placements, rotation, team working (projects), observation/site visits, discussion forums

Informal Channels
- Events, parties, celebrations
- Social networks/discussion forums

Recognition/Reinforcement
- Communication of wins
- Rewards/treats

Purpose

Although the AM is a major conduit for added-value knowledge and insight transference within his/her district, (s)he should also facilitate the swapping of ideas between GMs and units through multiple mechanisms. This framework surfaces a number of avenues through which AMs can encourage explicit/tacit knowledge diffusion across their district, leveraging the 'talents of all the team'. It must be said that the AM has really succeeded in this area when his/her subordinates swap ideas, information and knowledge independently without the AM's direct supervision!

Components and Principles

The means by which AMs can facilitate knowledge transfer are as follows:

1. *Architecture* – the structural design of the district enabling knowledge transference between parties through geographical sub-division (clusters, families, 'hub and spoke' and stores of excellence) and/or process responsibility allocation (leads, champions and experts)
2. *Formal Channels* – planned, set-piece team or one-to-one interactions that foster information exchange (such as district meetings, placements, observational visits, rotation, team working, projects and electronic discussion forums)
3. *Informal Channels* – relaxed, unregulated environments where tacit (uncodified, deep knowledge) can be shared (such as events, parties, celebrations and social networks)

4. *Recognition/Reinforcement* – regular communications that showcase and recognise best practice, highlighting its positive contribution to business growth/sustainability.

Issues

- **Blockages** – there are a number of blockages to knowledge transfer at an operational level in MUEs, not least the fact that as units 'compete' against one another with regards to league-table placing (on sales, profit, compliance, customer satisfaction, employee engagement etc.) some GMs will resort to hoarding or hiding the knowledge/insights that they believe sustain their competitive advantage over their peers.
- **Internal Focus** – this model is focused upon knowledge transfer between internal parties in a singular context. AMs must also explore for greater knowledge – seeking insights from competitors through a variety of means (visits, reading, contacts and networks etc.) – and encourage their GMs to do the same. Recycling tired old ideas internally or approaching problems with 'groupthink' solutions is not a way to forge ahead.

How AMs can use this Model

AMs should examine all knowledge transference channels within their district and determine what gaps they need to fill and what new mechanisms they should put in place to encourage facilitated or *spontaneous* sharing!

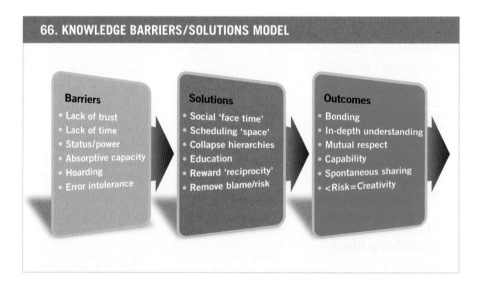

Purpose

The previous model highlighted mechanisms which the AM could use to facilitate knowledge transfer across his/her district. This inter-linked framework examines the common barriers encountered by managers trying to foster knowledge exchange, matching them against relevant solutions and key outcomes. As such, the model will help AMs to address specific roadblocks with tailored antidotes.

Components and Principles

The barriers to knowledge transfer highlighted in the framework can be addressed as follows:

1. *Lack of Trust* (i.e. a belief amongst innovators that their ideas might be diluted or stolen without reciprocation) – solutions include face-to-face communications/interaction (meetings, conferences, store visits etc.); namely, social 'face time' that will lead to bonding.
2. *Lack of Time* (i.e. distance and BAU activities prevent transmission) – here AMs should create time and space for idea exchange. Smarter methods require deployment for instant communication (such as digitally) which will facilitate swifter access to knowledge.
3. *Status/Power* (i.e. time servers and senior operators refuse to share with newbies) – create a set of values that stresses inclusivity, respect and sharing. Make ideas transcend status.
4. *Absorptive Capacity* – (i.e. personnel don't have the mental capacity to absorb/understand new ideas) – educate those that are willing but can't do; exit those that are unwilling and can't do. Use district expert and leads to expand capability through tailored training (show, not just lecture/tell).
5. *Knowledge Hoarding* (i.e. innovators jealously guard ideas for reasons of internal competitive advantage) – reward/recognise the sellers or purveyors of knowledge and encourage reciprocity between parties through social capital.
6. *Error Intolerance* (i.e. a belief among innovators that if their ideas fail to work elsewhere they will become coerced into stopping themselves) – remove gameplay, blame, sanction and retribution. Make it ok to try and fail. Create an environment in which people seek forgiveness rather than permission.

Issues

- **Identifying Blockages** – AMs will look for barriers but will often locate symptoms (ossification and inertia) rather than their causes. AMs 'mine deeply' in order to understand/rectify behavioural issues.
- **Lack of Humility** – AMs who encourage tacit knowledge disclosure and then appropriate ideas as their own – boasting to peers and superiors – lack humility and will quickly lose followership.

How AMs can use this Model

AMs should ask themselves why their subordinates aren't sharing knowledge and insights. Why does a lack of reciprocation, indebtedness and mutuality exist? What are the blockages? By identifying two or three major barriers (for instance, hoarding and error intolerance) they can apply appropriate solutions (e.g. reward sellers and grant permission to subordinates to try and fail).

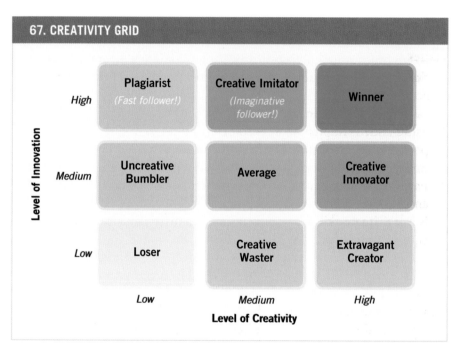

67. CREATIVITY GRID

	Low	Medium	High
High	Plagiarist *(Fast follower!)*	Creative Imitator *(Imaginative follower!)*	Winner
Medium	Uncreative Bumbler	Average	Creative Innovator
Low	Loser	Creative Waster	Extravagant Creator

Level of Innovation (vertical axis) — Level of Creativity (horizontal axis)

Purpose

The Creativity Grid[33] enables AMs to place their people in terms of their levels of creativity (imagination) and innovation (implementation). By juxtaposing the relationship between these two features, the AM can identify those who are genuinely creative and innovative (termed 'winners') and those at the other end of the spectrum (termed 'losers').

Components and Principles

The grid basically subdivides individuals into two types:

1. *High Value-added Types*

'*Winners*' – generate impactful ideas and make them happen

33 Majaro, S. (1988) *Management Ideas for Profit: the Creative Gap*, McGraw-Hill.

'Imitators' – harvest ideas and implement them
'Plagiarists' – scanners who copy and instigate
'Average' – display median levels of creativity/innovation
'Creatives' – generate great ideas and land some of them

2. ***Resource and Time Wasters***
   'Extravagants' – uncommercial idealists
   'Wasters' – daydreamers
   'Bumblers' – blaggers and time wasters
   'Losers' – useless!

Issues

- **Static** – this model assumes that individuals can be pigeonholed according to their relative levels of creativity and innovation. This assumes that people cannot be taught to think creatively to produce value-added, implementable solutions. Contrary evidence exists that people can – indeed – be taught to think differently, given the right mindset, tools and techniques.
- **Fast Followers** – the model has rather patronising labels like 'plagiarists' and 'imitators' but the art of copying (or so-called 'reverse engineering') is a legitimate skill that helps many organisations sustain competitive equity, if not advantage!

How AMs can use this Model

Assess (based on observable actions) where subordinates fit within this grid. Utilise the talents of those in the 'value-added' boxes and dismiss/ignore the contributions of those in the 'resource or time waster' cluster!

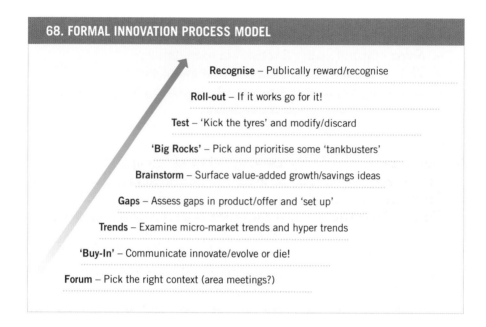

68. FORMAL INNOVATION PROCESS MODEL

Recognise – Publically reward/recognise

Roll-out – If it works go for it!

Test – 'Kick the tyres' and modify/discard

'Big Rocks' – Pick and prioritise some 'tankbusters'

Brainstorm – Surface value-added growth/savings ideas

Gaps – Assess gaps in product/offer and 'set up'

Trends – Examine micro-market trends and hyper trends

'Buy-In' – Communicate innovate/evolve or die!

Forum – Pick the right context (area meetings?)

Purpose

The Formal Innovation Process Model (FIPM) provides a checklist that AMs can use to focus their GMs and teams on generating and landing value-added ideas that address particular problems or opportunities within the district. Although slightly mechanistic, the FIPM is a useful way of getting all members of the team attuned to the notion that accepting the status quo is unacceptable in the face of innovative competition. It also gives team members a sense that they can add value locally in order to shape their commercial destinies (there is nothing that GMs discuss more than how they can increase sales).

Components and Principles

The FIPM outlines a sequential process incorporating the following steps:
- **Forum** – district meeting, away day or conference (try and break up the familiarity of surroundings)
- **Buy-in** – communicate the 'innovate or die' imperative (without paralysing discussion!)
- **Trends** – examine local consumer and competitor trends, insights and developments
- **Gaps** – surface gaps in current offer/systems/processes and potential opportunities
- **Brainstorm** – surface value-added ideas (allow both the group and individuals time to think of ideas; because of 'groupthink' and the

tendency to take polarised positions, large groups are not necessarily the best forum for coming up with ideas)
- *Select* – identify and prioritise 'big rock' runners
- *Test* – pilot, measure, review and improve in store
- *Roll Out* – implement if successful (timetable and resource it)
- *Recognise* – reward and communicate.

Issues

- **'Social Loafing' and 'Bystanding'** – in large groups, some members have a tendency to hide or make minimal/irrelevant contributions. Challenge them! Get them to present on one of the group's ideas!
- **Unconscious Mind** – what the model doesn't account for is the fact that feverish, conscious problem solving and creative thinking must be accompanied by periods of distracting downtime. Such periods of mind rest enables the brain to exercise an unconscious deliberation of the issue/challenge. Moments of clarity and inspiration will be derived from doing other things rather than sitting around a flip chart.

How AMs can use this Model

Many district meetings conducted by AMs have a backwards-looking financial performance and compliance focus. AMs must get through the hygiene stuff quickly and move the team onto how they can accelerate performance going forwards; the FIPM can be used for a session during the meeting to get people focused on creativity and innovation.

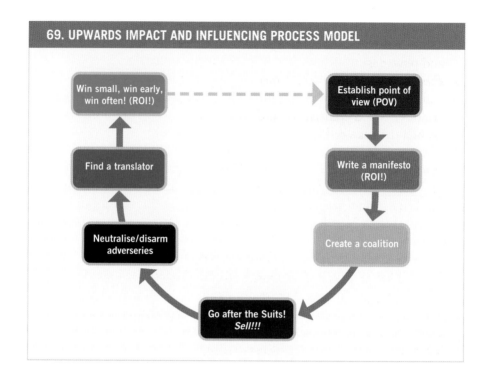

69. UPWARDS IMPACT AND INFLUENCING PROCESS MODEL

Win small, win early, win often! (ROI!)

Establish point of view (POV)

Find a translator

Write a manifesto (ROI!)

Neutralise/disarm adverseries

Create a coalition

Go after the Suits! *Sell!!!*

Purpose
This model[34] provides some insights into how AMs, their peers and teams can influence upwards within the organisation to evolve any part of the marketing mix. It provides a sequential framework that can act as a useful route map for AMs who are motivated to change things but have failed to achieve individual momentum.

Components and Principles
The sub-components of this model are as follows:
1. *Establish a Point of View* (POV) – create a credible, coherent, compelling and commercial POV based on hard data.
2. *Write a Manifesto* – infect others with your ideas. Capture their imagination with a picture of how you can resolve their discomfort.
3. *Create a Coalition* – assemble a group of colleagues who share your vision and passion. Present yourselves as a coordinated group speaking in a coordinated voice.
4. *Go after the Suits* – pick your targets. Find some that are searching for new ideas and, if necessary, bend your ideals a bit to fit the goals.

---

34 Adapted from Hamel, G. (2000) 'Waking Up IBM: How a Gang of Unlikely Rebels Transformed Big Blue', *Harvard Business Review*, May–June, pp.119–28.

5. *Neutralise* – disarm and co-opt adversaries rather than humiliating and demeaning them. Reciprocity wins converts; ranting leaves you isolated and powerless.
6. *Find a Translator* – find someone who can build a bridge between you and the people in power. Senior staffers and newly appointed executives are often good translator candidates – they're usually hungry for an agenda they can call their own.
7. *Win small, Win early, Win often!* – Demonstrate that your ideas actually work and have a real ROI. Start small. As your record of wins grows longer, you'll find it easier to make the transition from an isolated initiative to an integral part of the business.

Issues

- **Capacity** – in many ways, this model is very idealistic: a group of likeminded innovators/visionaries banding together to sell their value-added ideas to senior policy makers and/or resource holders! How are AMs expected to have the energy and extra capacity to do this given the extraordinary demands of the role?
- **Thieves!** – one risk this process carries is that having 'translated', the supportive suits will claim total credit, leaving the originators disillusioned and demotivated.

How AMs can use this Model

In order to widely diffuse great ideas that are generated 'on the ground', this process provides a useful route map as to how AMs can impact and influence upwards. The key point to make (to allay a frequent complaint made by senior managers that are bombarded by 'enthusiasts') is that any proposal that is taken up the chain has to have a fully costed ROI. In order to get traction in the boardroom, learn to speak the language of board members (which is usually conducted through the figures).

SECTION 5

AM PERSONAL CHARACTERISTICS

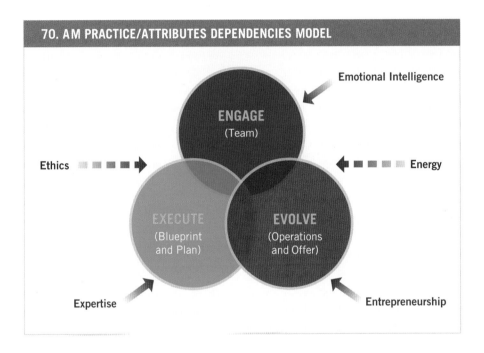

70. AM PRACTICE/ATTRIBUTES DEPENDENCIES MODEL

The previous sections outlined models that AMs can use in order to improve their professional practice. Clearly the AM requires a number of job-related skills and competencies to expedite this role – but what are the personal characteristics of effective AMs? What attributes and associated behaviours are required for the effective discharge of this highly complex and ambiguous role? Through what means can these characteristics be developed? The Integrated Model of Area Management (Model 15) outlined practices and attributes that require the successful exposition of this role; this section will examine each essential attribute in turn.

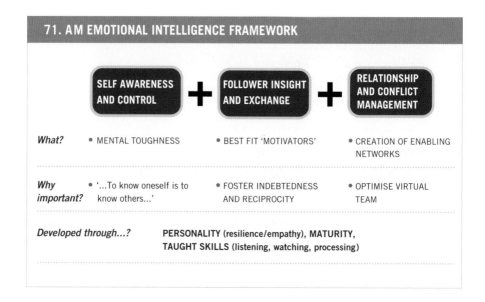

71. AM EMOTIONAL INTELLIGENCE FRAMEWORK

SELF AWARENESS AND CONTROL + **FOLLOWER INSIGHT AND EXCHANGE** + **RELATIONSHIP AND CONFLICT MANAGEMENT**

	SELF AWARENESS AND CONTROL	FOLLOWER INSIGHT AND EXCHANGE	RELATIONSHIP AND CONFLICT MANAGEMENT
What?	• MENTAL TOUGHNESS	• BEST FIT 'MOTIVATORS'	• CREATION OF ENABLING NETWORKS
Why important?	• '...To know oneself is to know others...'	• FOSTER INDEBTEDNESS AND RECIPROCITY	• OPTIMISE VIRTUAL TEAM

Developed through...? PERSONALITY (resilience/empathy), MATURITY, TAUGHT SKILLS (listening, watching, processing)

Given the importance of *engaging* followers in service-based MUEs, it is unsurprising that the first major characteristic of effective AMs is emotional intelligence (EI). This is defined generally within the academic literature as an ability, skill or perceived ability to identify, assess and control the emotions of oneself, others and groups. This characteristic (which comprises three dimensions: *self-awareness and control; follower insight and exchange*; and *relationship and conflict management*) will now be considered, followed by illustrations as to how it might be developed.

Self-awareness and Control

The combination of knowing oneself and exercising personal control through high levels of mental toughness is an important feature of effective AMs. Due to the workload and associated pressures/stresses of the role, effective MULs need to acquire a degree of self-knowledge and discipline with regards to how they react to certain situations, demonstrating a fair amount of manners and grace under immense provocation. Effective AMs demonstrate the following behaviours with regards to self-awareness and control:

Facets of Self-awareness and Control
- **Self-awareness through:**
  - Honest reflection
  - Desire for improvement
  - Ability to listen to feedback

- **Mental toughness through:**
  - Adapting to different challenges and circumstances
  - Emotional self-control under pressure
  - Balanced view of success and failure
  - Focus upon controlling the 'controllables'
  - Confidence in one's own abilities.

Follower Insight and Exchange

Self-awareness will undoubtedly help AMs – through the process of understanding 'self' – to read the motives/desires of their followers, guiding them as to which practices/approaches they should adopt with individuals/teams to induce reciprocity and indebtedness so that they can rely on high levels of operational excellence without direct daily supervision. With regard to awareness of others – in order to shape and control emotions – effective AMs display the following attributes:

Facets of Follower Insight
- Empathy – authentic questioning and listening skills
- Processing – ability to read/interpret the motives of others
- Fit – ability to apply the right currency of exchange.

This ability to gain follower insight is a skill that, based on my previous research, is more evident in female than male AMs. The ability to sense, understand and respond to the emotions/motives of others did not come naturally to a number of output-focused male AMs. Their tendency to 'talk at' their people rather than to listen and empathise was an inhibiting factor in gaining control of the emotions of others. This is a major inhibitor. Whilst the AM's capacity to understand the attitudes, disposition and motivations of their followers – in order to lead to them to the achievement of assured operational outcomes – is an important entry point, it is the AM's skill in adapting/fitting the right exchange mechanisms to the right person/team that will ultimately determine value-added reciprocity-based behaviour:

Facets of Follower Exchange
- Understand – locate follower needs/desires through:
  - Listening to stories and observing real behaviours/outcomes
- Apply guile and nous – fit currencies of exchange through:
  - Judging personality, attitude, capability and situation
  - Ensuring the *costs* of follower roles are compensated by *benefits* that lead to positive *outcomes* (benefits – costs = outcomes)

○ Creating win–win solutions for both the AM and GM
- Monitor outcomes – constantly review desired outputs:
  ○ Operational excellence without direct daily supervision.

Relationship and Conflict Management

As stated, it is the natural inclination of many AMs to 'go native', disassociating themselves from the rest of the wider organisation in the misplaced belief that it is out to get them. Such a position is not only immature and ultimately self-defeating; it also has a negative impact on performance by closing off access to valuable information and potential support mechanisms. Thus, in addition to self-awareness and follower insight, effective AMs are adept at fostering and maintaining good relationships across the organisation. Effective AMs are able to deal with ambiguity, understanding that most organisations are riven by competing interests and that they can only control the controllables. In the absence of having the power and influence to prevent conflict between the operational line and, for instance, parts of the technocracy such as Property or Marketing, they focus upon getting the very best outcomes possible in difficult situations. Within their own orbit of control, they use the techniques and methods outlined above, the most significant weapon being the creation of win–win outcomes through the process of social exchange with support staff:

Facets of Relationship and Conflict Management
- Creation of 'enabling' networks through:
  ○ Spending time at the centre (either job role or networking)
  ○ Telephoning and meeting peers
  ○ Volunteering for project work and task forces
- Transparency and honesty during dealings (limiting game play)
- Asking for help from others and/or involving others in solutions (recognising their contribution)
- Creating win–win situations through social exchange (help support staff to attain own goals).

Developing AM EI

How do MUEs develop EI amongst AMs? Changing or modifying behaviours which are connected to personality and prior socialisation is notoriously difficult, unless the recipients are open to honest feedback which they are prepared to incorporate into alternative ways of working. MUEs can help AMs to understand their levels of resilience/self-control and their impact upon others (followers, peers and stakeholders) but it is a matter of individual preparedness to change which is key.

Developing AM Emotional Intelligence

- Measure current position:
  - 360 degree, MTQ48, observation, previous data (PDP feedback, employee engagement etc.)
- Behavioural interventions:
  - Coaching/mentoring

Field-based observation and feedback
  - Modelling from exemplars
  - Classroom simulation
  - Reflective logs
  - Placement on central project teams/secondments/rotation.

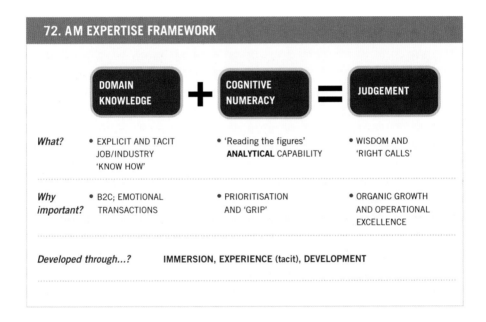

Expertise – the technical skills and knowledge applied in an impactful manner within the AM practice domain – is the second personal characteristic of the effective AM (highly connected to **executing** the blueprint and plan). From a general academic view, there are two main approaches to understanding expertise: first, the *communities of practice* and, second, the *individual expert capacity* view. The former sees expertise as a socially constructed phenomenon where narratives and bias for action are shaped by groups, enabling members to codify, transfer and enact expertise within specific domains. Problems pointed out by this domain relate to the emergence of 'groupthink' and isometric convergence that stifles original thinking. The latter defines expertise as an innate characteristic of individuals which is formed as a result of absorptive capacity, environmental context, and continuous and deliberate practice. Achieving expertise in certain fields or domains has been estimated by some commentators to involve 10,000 hours or a period of five years of complete immersion. With specific reference to effective AMs, expertise manifests itself along three dimensions: *domain knowledge* and *professional practice/numeracy* which both lead to a high level of *confidence/judgement*.

Domain Knowledge

Within organisations, knowledge manifests itself in both explicit and tacit form. *Explicit knowledge* is expressed formally, being transferred through mechanisms such as written instruction and/or verbal communication. By contrast, *tacit knowledge* is difficult to transfer as it comprises informal habits and cultural idiosyncrasies that people and organisations are often unaware they possess or how it provides inimitable added value. Dissemination of this form of knowledge requires a high degree of trust-based personal contact and interaction.

A major characteristic of effective AMs is *explicit* domain knowledge of the sector, organisation and job. Thus, effective AMs will be successful in comparison to their peers through familiarisation and deep understanding of the following:

Facets of Domain Knowledge
- Service-sector familiarity
  - Business-to-consumer transactions
- Organisational dynamics
  - Strategy/structure/culture
  - Supply chain
- Product/brand understanding
  - Positioning (value, mid or premium)
  - Functional/emotional drivers (people, promotion, place, pricing etc.)
- Blueprint mastery
  - Operational systems
    - Labour processes, standard operating procedures, availability, stock & waste procedures, sales & pricing monitoring, due diligence and essential maintenance processes, ad hoc processes/change initiatives
  - Brand standards

- Merchandising & display, internal environmental 'sensory' management, external environment
  - Service delivery mechanisms
    - HRM, service concept adherence, customer feedback follow-up, service promise & complaints resolution.

Cognitive Numeracy

Effective AMs will be successful in comparison to their peers in the achievement of many of their company-set objectives through domain knowledge. But it is not only their explicit knowledge of what matters that counts; rather, it is their *tacit* knowledge of 'how to do it' that separates them from the norm. In particular, effective AMs possess extensive practice-based knowledge, combined with superior *cognitive* thinking skills (highly connected to financial acuity), which enable them to unscramble how they can increase portfolio/unit performance – in spite of a wide span of control issues.

For instance, in the case of district and unit P&Ls, AMs are presented with a voluminous amount of information. How do they discriminate between the most significant data sets and indicators and, more importantly, focus upon what do they need to do to improve performance? The answer is that they apply a high level of cognitive reasoning to a series of problematics arising from the P&L. Effective AMs are adept at locating patterns of dysfunctionality and/or opportunities to move the P&L in the right direction. These cognitive skills also apply to the prioritisation of measures, tasks and initiatives. However, although effective AMs involve their teams and local cluster champions in creating a local vision and prioritising /resolving certain challenges, the fact that accountability ultimately resides with them renders their ability to ensure that the *right things are being focused upon, at the right time, by the right people* (through a complex process of association and reasoning) as absolutely critical:

Facets of Numeracy/Professional Practice
- 'Reading the P&L'
  - Input–output dependencies and linkages
  - Identification of causal connections
- Direction, prioritisation and delegation
  - Local vision and clear direction
  - 80/20 Prioritisation ('big rocks')
  - Distributed delegation (leads, process champions, support staff 'enablers' etc.)

- 'Right person, right site, right time'
  - Ensure appropriate GM–site fit.

With regards to the latter point in the above table, the process of ensuring the right GM–site fit is crucial in MUEs with – as has already been stated – the right unit manager being estimated to add 10% in sales in a retail environment and up to 30% in leisure. Thus, fitting the appropriate GM to a vacant unit with inimitable local market dynamics (from both a labour and customer point of view) that melds and complements the district team is a non-trivial matter of professional judgement that is developed over a period of time.

Developing AM Expertise

The development interventions that apply to new/existing AMs will vary according to prior experience, capability and situation. As a start point, AMs will obviously have to master the basics of the domain in which they are being expected to operate – something that newly appointed GMs (should) already possess. However, once the explicit factors relating to the role have been mastered, great attention must be paid to the way in which AMs apply perception/reasoning to problems/opportunities within their districts:

Developing AM Expertise
- **Domain knowledge**
  - Systems/standards training/testing
    - Procedures and policies
    - Reportage and metrics
  - Immersion
    - OTJ/'back to the floor' training and development
    - 'Strawberry patches'/cluster responsibilities for AM potentials
- **Numeracy/professional practice**
  - Numerical/cognitive perception/reasoning training
    - Case studies and exercises that encompass:
      - Portfolio/unit data (quant./qual.) gathering/sifting
      - Location of insights/causal drivers
      - Patterns of dysfunctionality/opportunity
      - Remedial solutions/prioritisation
  - Planning, organising and delegation training (TO CREATE CAPACITY)
    - Portfolio strategy and planning
    - Scheduling, meetings and time management
    - Portfolio delegation.

Mastering both elements of expertise will lead to high levels of *judgement* and *confidence* amongst AMs, which will bolster their credibility amongst their peers and followers. The fact remains, however, that whilst most MUEs are good at the former element of expertise (basic domain development), they are generally lax in the latter (numeracy/professional practice), often throwing ex-GMs into the role with little training in diagnostics and problem solving/resolution in complex portfolio situations. Insufficient attention is paid by most MUEs to cognitive-thinking-skills development amongst AMs – a theme to which I will return below.

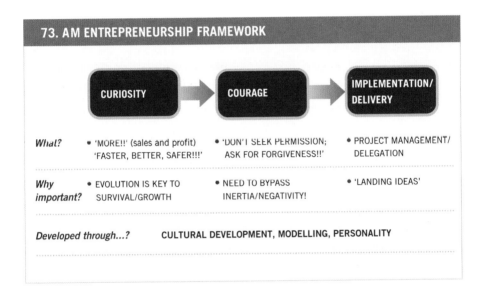

The next characteristic that effective AMs display is corporate entrepreneurship where – within a given framework – they relentlessly focus upon **evolving** operations and the offer, doing things 'quicker, smarter and better'. Classically, corporate innovators have been termed 'intrapreneurs', implying that – given existing constraints – they think and act differently from their non-corporate 'maverick' entrepreneurial cousins. This is manifestly not the case. The kind of behaviours that entrepreneurs display – constant challenging of orthodoxy and a courageous desire to create something innovative – are characteristics that are shared by corporate entrepreneurs, albeit they have to innovate in more bounded environments. Indeed, one advantage that corporate entrepreneurs have is the 'hard' and 'soft' resources to trial new products and methods of working. Obviously their job is made easier if organisations recognise the benefits of bottom-up innovation, creating space for NPD and encouraging/capturing value-added insights through feedback loops and recognition. But what dimensions of entrepreneurship apply to AMs? What are the sub-components needed for its successful exposition?

Curiosity and Courage

In both hard and soft branded MUEs, it is an incontrovertible fact that, due to a number of legacy-related and/or contextual factors, *every site is different*. Sites are rarely *completely* homogenous in terms of position, scale, layout, officialdom, customer demographics and labour markets. This represents a major opportunity for the effective AM to make local iterations (where permissible) to processes, configuration, offer, range, pricing, promotions, local PR and rates of pay in order to leverage sales. In order to do this, however, the effective MSM needs appropriate levels of *curiosity* which enables him/her to **see the differences**. In addition, (s)he needs the appropriate level of *courage* and *relentless persistence* to drive/permit *legal* improvements (i.e. adaptations that are not going to blow up the machine or result in gorging) both in single sites and/or across the portfolio.

Facets of AM Curiosity and Courage
- Natural inquisitiveness about:
  o How well things work for staff AND customers
  o How things can be done better to reduce costs or increase sales
- Ability to 'SEE THE DIFFERENCES' in each site:
  o I.e. processes, layout, range, promotion, events (social media)
- Courage to try new things:
  o 'Don't ask for permission, ask for forgiveness'.

Implementation and Delivery

The difficulty facing naturally innovative and inquisitive AMs is how they land added-value ideas that emerge from one unit, across their portfolios. For sure, they can assign responsibility for knowledge transfer and delivery to their nominated process champions and leads but how do they facilitate more organic means of transmission/adoption? The answer to this is that effective AMs will encourage knowledge transference across their portfolios by breaking hoarding behaviours (i.e. the possessors of useful knowledge refusing to share insights due to their competitive advantage) through encouraging reciprocity and universal mutual gain. The forum through which such sharing can be encouraged and engineered (particularly in managed/franchised environments) is during district meetings where effective AMs, having dealt with the compliance stuff (i.e. labour, other costs, and health and safety) during weekly teleconference or Skype calls, will concentrate on improvement and innovation.

Facets of Implementation and Delivery
- Process capability to deliver and land things
  - Utilise process leads and champions
- Knowledge transfer mechanisms to break hoarding
  - Events, conferences, rotations, placements, 'sitting-with-nellie', communities of practice (clusters etc.).

Developing AM Entrepreneurship

How do MUEs encourage entrepreneurship amongst their AM population? AMs have generally been promoted from GM level for their technical proficiency rather than cognitive thinking skills. Additionally, those that have been genuinely innovative in-store have not (unless they have been assigned to do so) been responsible for spreading ideas over a distance, across a portfolio of sites. What MUEs need to do, therefore, is ensure their AM population has a sufficient level of courage and critical thinking to 'try new things', in addition to understanding the mechanisms through which they can encourage cross-portfolio knowledge transmission.

Developing AM Entrepreneurship
- Senior role-modelling:
  - Construction/demonstrations of 'freedom within a frame'
  - Public recognition of innovation/process improvement
  - Permission to try and fail (remove penalties/sanctions)
- Measure AM current position:
  - Psychometric profiling (MINDSET, curiosity, persistence and courage), previous evidence of innovating/risk taking, problem-solving skills
- Development interventions:
  - Brainstorming tools/OPI (Operational Improvement and Innovation) techniques/case study examples
  - Portfolio knowledge transfer training:
    - Process leads and champions, meetings and events etc.
- Impact and influencing skills training:
  - How to transmit ideas upwards to senior policy-makers.

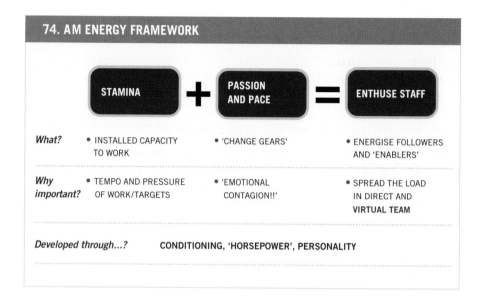

74. AM ENERGY FRAMEWORK

	STAMINA	+	PASSION AND PACE	=	ENTHUSE STAFF
What?	• INSTALLED CAPACITY TO WORK		• 'CHANGE GEARS'		• ENERGISE FOLLOWERS AND 'ENABLERS'
Why important?	• TEMPO AND PRESSURE OF WORK/TARGETS		• 'EMOTIONAL CONTAGION!!'		• SPREAD THE LOAD IN DIRECT AND VIRTUAL TEAM
Developed through...?			CONDITIONING, 'HORSEPOWER', PERSONALITY		

EI, expertise and entrepreneurship are critical components in the makeup of the effective AM (linked directly to engage, execute and evolve practices) but they will be diluted, potentially rendered irrelevant, unless AMs have high energy levels. Given the aforementioned challenges and stresses of the role – derived from geographical, span of control and positional pressures – effective AMs require significant reserves of energy to overcome interference in order to get the job done. What are the critical dimensions of this construct with regards to AMs?

Stamina

The 24/7 nature of the AM role dictates that they must have high levels of stamina/'installed capacity' to work in order to cope with the demands of the role. In academic terms, stamina or physical energy is typically defined as the ability to sustain a prolonged physical or mental effort. Rituals such as nutrition, exercise, sleep and rest have a positive correlation with increased work capacity, engagement and motivation. Such habits are regarded by some commentators as one of the most effective ways of controlling and reducing stressors. The reality, however, is that given the demands and intractable conundrums faced by most AMs on a day-to-day basis, few have the time or space to achieve physical or spiritual balance. Whilst a limited amount of stress is seen as a useful performance enhancer in certain circumstances, constant burdensome demands on the AM can sap stamina, eventually leading to declining levels of discretionary effort, high intention-to-quit rates and, in extreme cases, absence, sickness and burn out.

But why do AMs require such large reserves of stamina?

Factors Requiring AM Stamina
- Physical distance from units
- BAU activity execution:
  - Operational excellence
  - Application of professional practice
- Ad-hoc initiatives:
  - Organisation change
  - Refurbishments and new openings
  - Product pilots/launches
  - Troubleshooting/firefighting.

There is little doubt that the AM role can, with its large amount of sedentary travel between units and unusual working hours, promote an exceptionally unhealthy lifestyle. Why? In part, the answer lies in the addictive nature of the job, the fact that AMs become, in the words of one respondent, 'email junkies and iPhone addicts'. To a certain extent, the addictive nature of the job (where there is no end to the number of tasks that need completing or problems that require resolution) provides constant affirmation of their identity – that they are needed and important!

Passion and Pace

MUEs are 'people' businesses where AMs need to convey infectious enthusiasm and a 'can-do' attitude that engages and motivates their direct (line) and indirect (virtual support) teams, who – in turn – will enthuse their customers. Within the academic literature, *passion* is typically conceived of as *personal commitment*, high levels of which are thought to be achieved through job role fit, goal alignment and HRM practice interventions (i.e. development, reward, communication and involvement). It is also linked to levels of *positive energy*, which is conceptualised as helping people to perform at their best through techniques such as 'expressing appreciation to others' thereby fuelling 'positive emotions'. In addition, conveying passion is inextricably linked to *pace* and urgency. Given the service orientation of MUEs where the frontline staff is expected to respond immediately and sympathetically to customer demands, effective AMs set the 'dynamic tone' by dispatching tasks and requests quickly and efficiently. The importance of pace is recognised by academic commentators, most notably by Belbin (see Model 32 – Team Development) who argued that organisations and teams require 'completer finishers' (a prime requirement of field-based operatives in MUEs) alongside other actors, in order to ensure that tasks were implemented on time, to specification.

Facets behind Passion and Pace
- Passion and 'emotional contagion' through:
  - Humour, fun and enjoyment
  - Infectious enthusiasm
  - Cheerleading success
  - Visibility and positivity
  - 'Changing gears' (according to season, event, trading session etc.)
- Pace and urgency through:
  - Anticipating and acting upon issues swiftly
  - Quick responses to requests (promissory speed)
  - Progress chasing/implementation
  - Answering emails and iPhone messages regularly
  - Following up on promises
  - Turning around work swiftly and efficiently.

Going back to passion, it is important to state that its conveyance has positive effects both ways. AMs derive much of their inspiration and energy from the passion of their people; site visits often served a re-energising need for themselves. Given the somewhat isolated home-working environment of their role and stifling demands of the centre, AMs often find site visits refreshing and motivational. Seeing the positive outcomes of appointments that they have made and the successes of their people reinforces their sense of passion for the job.

Developing AM Energy
Inevitably, individual reserves of AM energy are connected to work ethic, attitude, personality and situation (i.e. the ebb and flow of central diktats and demands). But what can MUEs do to develop and enhance levels of energy?

Developing AM Energy
- Measure current position:
  - Personal productivity (level/speed of tasks despatched, number of store visits etc.)
  - Staff engagement and customer satisfaction
- Behavioural interventions:
  - 'Wellness' programmes
    - Medical check-ups
    - Rules on work hours, travel, iPhones and laptop/tablet use

- Managerial skills training (creating capacity):
  - Planning, prioritising, organising and delegating
- Technical interventions:
  - Architecture
    - Store numbers and geography
    - Nominated support staff support
  - Process efficiency
    - Machinery, technology and facilities that work
    - Procedural and process SIMPLICITY
    - Appropriate staff training systems.

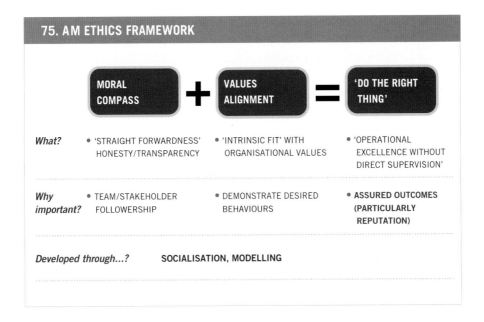

75. AM ETHICS FRAMEWORK

| | MORAL COMPASS | + | VALUES ALIGNMENT | = | 'DO THE RIGHT THING' |

	MORAL COMPASS	VALUES ALIGNMENT	'DO THE RIGHT THING'
What?	'STRAIGHT FORWARDNESS' HONESTY/TRANSPARENCY	'INTRINSIC FIT' WITH ORGANISATIONAL VALUES	'OPERATIONAL EXCELLENCE WITHOUT DIRECT SUPERVISION'
Why important?	TEAM/STAKEHOLDER FOLLOWERSHIP	DEMONSTRATE DESIRED BEHAVIOURS	ASSURED OUTCOMES (PARTICULARLY REPUTATION)
Developed through...?	SOCIALISATION, MODELLING		

The field of business ethics has received considerable attention over the past few years in developed contexts, not least due to the dubious behaviours of bankers which contributed to the 2008 financial collapse in the 'West', which occurred in spite of previous attempts by policy makers to instil legal codes of permitted behaviour (e.g. Sarbannes Oxley in the United States). MUEs like other corporate entities all have CSR and compliance frameworks that define rights and obligations which should govern relations between themselves and their stakeholders. In particular, employees are prescribed ethical obligations to their organisations, such as reporting malfeasance through whistleblowing. The issue in MUEs is, how – given the dispersed multi-site nature of the organisational entity – organisations are to regulate behaviours effectively. In this respect, they are highly reliant on their field-based AMs to conform to their codes of ethics.

The foundation of ethical behaviour is sound *morals* – meaning the ability to act 'properly' in a good way. Essentially, individual morality is derived from ethical social mores enshrined in *societal* and cultural *values*. Previous reference has been made to how values are imprinted upon individuals through conditioning and socialisation at a very early age through parenting, education and peer-group influences. There are two issues for AMs: first, how do they ensure their own *personal morality* is aligned to that of the MUE? and second, how do they influence and regulate the *value-sets* of those around them?

As regards the first question, AMs in MUEs will sometimes be placed in situations where they are faced with seemingly intractable decisions. Given their distance from the centre and the demands placed upon them to hit certain financial targets, should they cheat (e.g. bribe officials or falsify data/accounts) to get ahead? Also – in certain high-context cultures – should they accede to local customs, favouring relationships above performance and asserting their authority in a self-protective manner? Here, unlearning poor practice, self-regulation and *moral control* amongst AMs are particularly important to 'doing the right thing'. In respect of others, the AM has a huge role to play in modelling MUE *values* – especially in relation to followers. For instance, Generation Y and (upcoming) millennials are portrayed as having different aspirations and value sets from previous generations. Their conception of work is less 'dutiful cradle to grave', rather more as 'a means to an end' – work providing income for extra-curricular social activities. The AM, therefore, has a key role in ensuring that the value sets of MUEs are inculcated into younger workers who have not been previously conditioned to accept some quite basic norms (standards, timekeeping, appearance, behaviour etc.).

Facets of AM Ethics
- 'Doing the right thing' as well as 'doing it right'
- Acting authentically through:
  o Consistent, balanced and mature behaviours
  o Honest and open communications
- Fairness and equity through:
  o No favouritism/nepotism
  o Balanced adjudication on misdemeanours.

Developing AM Ethics
The question for MUEs is how to ensure their values transcend personal/local cultural values where there are clear disjunctures. More

succinctly, how can they ensure their AMs have sufficiently robust moral compasses and that their organisational values are accepted and enacted by individuals who might be conditioned to operate according to a contrary set of values (especially amongst Generation Y workers)?

How to Develop AM Ethics
- Measure current position:
  - Test ethics through psychometrics
  - Analyse patterns of previous decision making
  - Check on previous behaviour – talk to subordinates; analyse employee engagement scores on trust
  - Observe during a trial period of employment
- Interventions:
  - Modelling – socialisation through 'leader' values modelling
  - Benefit upselling – sell the upsides (i.e. how organisational values result in positive personal outcomes for individuals in terms of meritocratic progression, reputation etc.)
  - Coherent logic – ensure coherent logic prevails for value set.

Alphabetical Index of Models